SHADOWS
on the WALL

To: Tom,
I Hope you Enjoy my
Stories...

One
Policeman's
Journey

DENNIS J. CRONIN

outskirts
press

Dedication

This book is dedicated to the brave men and women of law enforcement who put their lives on the line every day to protect and serve.

ACKNOWLEDGEMENTS

First and foremost, I want to express my deepest gratitude to my beautiful wife, Kathleen, who has spent countless hours by my side. She encouraged and helped me to finish this project and get through some of the more difficult incidents that have happened in my life. Secondly, I would like to thank Carol Dioguardi for her patience, time, and word-smithing ability that helped me complete this work. Finally, I would like to thank all of my family and friends who have also been by my side. They allowed me to tell my stories count-less times and urged me to put them down on paper.

TABLE OF CONTENTS

INTRODUCTION

The stories that you are about to read are based on actual events that have helped define my life. The names of the officers, including my own, have been changed, as well as the name of the town and different places mentioned, but the stories are real and are told the way I remember them. They represent just a small fraction of events that have occurred throughout my almost thirty-seven-year career of wearing a badge.

When I started my career over fifty years ago, the world was a different place. Police officers were respected and life was a bit simpler. The technology was very different because we didn't have cell phones until the 1990s and body cameras were nonexistent. The population of the town was much smaller, which allowed us to develop relationships with our community's residents. For example, if a local was caught driving on the road while under the influence of alcohol, we could take the keys away and drive that person home. Obviously, because of liability issues, that can no longer be done today. If we responded to a house BBQ because of a noise complaint, it was typical for the owners to lower the music and then invite us in for a cold soda and a burger. We were often waved to as we patrolled neighborhoods and we could stop and talk to residents. The people always knew that they could depend on us when needed.

In the early days on the job, we weren't viewed so severely and watched under a microscope. To ascertain information, we were able to use unconventional methods that are now unacceptable in today's society. With police protocols changing every day and the controversial issues of whose lives matter, the more than 900,000 current law enforcement officers in our country have a very difficult and dangerous job. I hope when you are done reading this book, you will have a better understanding of the humanization of what one police officer went through during his career.

CHAPTER 1
THE JOURNEY BEGINS

My name is Dennis Russell. This is the story of my life as a police officer. I carried a badge for almost thirty-seven years. When I began, the war in Viet Nam was nearing its peak and young men and women, including many of my friends, were heading into harm's way thousands of miles from home. Fortunately, God had other plans for me and my journey was about to begin.

It was the summer of 1968, I had just finished college, and my plans for the future were pretty well set. My college roommate was Peter Swenson, whose family owned a multi-million-dollar import export company. The company was called *Swenson's Nordic Foods* and was based out of Oslo, Norway with an office in Boston, Massachusetts. Pete had asked me to join the company as his advertising consultant. I felt this was the perfect opportunity for me to advance my career in a field that I loved. We had planned this business partnership since our first year together and now it was finally going to come true. Pete's grandfather was retiring and his father, Michael, was taking over the company. My life seemed to be set, but all that was about to change.

With these plans in mind, I asked for a family meeting. Whenever we had a major decision to make, we called this type of meeting. My father was a U.S. Postal Inspector with the Jefferson Township Post Office. His fondest hope was that I would carry on in the family's footsteps, since both of his brothers were police officers and their four sons were police officers, as well. It was almost a mandate that I would become one, too, but this was the farthest thing from my mind. I had seen firsthand the stress and worry that profession had put on my relatives and knew it was not for me. I wanted a more normal life; one where, when I left for work, there was an excellent chance I would return. I also wanted a family life that meant my wife wouldn't grow old before her time from not knowing whether I would come home safe and in one piece, and my children wouldn't have to ask if Dad would be there for Christmas, graduations, birthdays, and vacations. My problem laid within my love for my father; there was nothing I wouldn't do for him. And right now, he wanted me to continue in the family's chosen field.

I'll never forget that July morning. It was almost ninety-five degrees at 11:00 am. As I walked into the Jefferson Township Police Department, I looked straight into the eyes of the desk sergeant and asked, "Where do I go to take the test for a police officer?" Six weeks later, I was standing in the office of the mayor with my hand raised, taking the Oath of Allegiance. As I looked around the room, my eyes caught my father. Tears were rolling down his face. He looked so proud as he held my mother's hand, but there was a completely different look on her face. It was a look of fear and concern, with a hint of pride. I knew my life would never be the same again.

CHAPTER 2
THE POLICE ACADEMY

It was an early morning drive from home to the academy. It was late September and a crisp morning; the weather was about fifty degrees and unseasonably cold for that time of year. As I pulled into the front gate of the academy, I was met by an officer telling me where to park my car. I didn't see that vehicle for the next two weeks because recruits weren't allowed to leave the base during those first few weeks. Since it was the first day of class, they gave us an easy day. It consisted of taking a class picture, getting an assignment to barracks, adjusting to a new environment, and meeting the other recruits and staff.

Upon entering the barracks, I saw it was a typical military-style building – a "U" shaped structure with long sides and bathrooms that connected them. Each side in a section had eleven beds and alongside each bed was a locker. We were split up into four groups, with twenty-two recruits in each section. After being assigned to our barracks, we were then each assigned a particular bed. At that point, the instructor, Sergeant Charlesworth, demonstrated to us the proper way of making a bed, with hospital corners and the ability to bounce a quarter off the top cover – and in his words, "It better bounce." He then showed us the right way to set up our lockers. There was to be no deviation from that or you would receive a gig, as he would call it, which was a demerit. If you received one, you would not be allowed to go home on a weekend unless you worked it off before 4:00 pm that Friday. My group was then marched to the bathroom area and instructed on the correct cleaning method for toilets, showers, floors, sinks, and mirrors. All of this was a lot to digest on the first day. We were then told to get on our Class A uniforms and muster in the street in front of the barracks. At this point, I didn't know what to expect, but it soon became very clear.

Looking at the faces and physiques of the eight training officers outside, I realized that they gave the appearance of being "poster boys" for the state police. There wasn't one instructor that was less than six feet tall. They had spit-shined shoes, their hair was tightly cropped, their hats were pulled down to where the brim was just two fingers above the nose, and their uniforms were impeccably tailored. The sight that disturbed me the most was that they all had this icy stare. It was almost as if instead of them looking at you, they were looking through you. Stepping out from the group of instructors was the commandant of the police academy. His name was Captain Mark Sampson. He had that same spit-and-polished look as the others. He wore numerous citations and hash marks on his sleeves. One could see very clearly that he was not a man to be trifled with. When he spoke, I could have sworn I heard thunder. He was also older than the other instructors. His face was more weather-beaten, gray in the temples, but still, there was that icy stare. When you looked at him, you knew he demanded respect. His words were few, but he made no mistake as to what he wanted.

We were then escorted into the auditorium, broken into eight groups. Each group was given a set of academy rules and regulations and our schedule for the next two weeks. They made it crystal clear that we should never be late and never change the schedule for any reason. After being dismissed, we returned to the barracks and started putting our new home in order. We had two more orientation classes that day before dinner. One of the major rules in the cafeteria was that you could have as much food as you wanted, but throw nothing in the garbage. Our trays had to be empty when we finished a meal. I didn't completely understand this rule, although I found out the hard way exactly what it meant – but that is another story. Sleep didn't come easily that night, even though I was mentally, physically, and emotionally exhausted. But the next day, if possible, was about to become worse.

Day two started normally but deteriorated rapidly. After breakfast, my first scheduled class was in Self Defense, or so I thought. Sometime during the previous night, one of the recruits in my group DOR'd (Dropped on Request), which means he left the academy. His first scheduled assignment would have been range duty. I was scheduled for the following day but because he had left, my schedule was then moved up and I became the range officer. However, they failed to notify me. As a result, I broke the major academy rule of never being late for a scheduled assignment. While I was in my Self Defense class, Trooper Taylor entered the room and asked, "Where is recruit

Russell?" Raising my hand, I replied, "Here, sir." The next few words were like a knife to the heart. He pointed out to me that the first rule of this academy was to never be late for an assignment. True, when recruit Cook DOR'd, I took on his schedule but was never informed that he had left. However, that had no bearing on me knowing where I should be. Just one of the rules that I had to learn the hard way. My relatives who were on the job had told me before entering the academy to never let the instructors learn your name early; otherwise, you would find yourself getting every dirty detail and being made an example of. Because of this scheduling mistake, I not only received three demerits, or gigs, but they now knew my name.

The problem with demerits, as I stated before, was that if you had accrued any during the week, they had to be worked off prior to leaving on Friday at 4:00 pm. To remove one demerit, you had to walk the quad for one half hour. The quad was a grassy area adjacent to the cafeteria. It was approximately one square acre. It had sidewalks on three sides and the front, or fourth, side was the main street at the academy. The dress code was full dress uniform, which consisted of your hat, your blouse with tie, your weapon with all leather gear, and your dress shoes. Walking in the sun for half an hour was unbearable on days when it was warm or hot. You could easily sweat off several pounds due to the fact that the uniform was black and heavy. On occasion, the entire group would receive one or more demerits based on specific offenses. One of the sadistic ways to motivate us when that happened was to take the entire group for a "stroll" along the beach. This meant you were going to run on the beach in your combat boots in the soft sand until someone threw up. This happened often in the early weeks to weed out the weaker candidates.

Through sheer accident, I found an alternative to working off demerits. One day after walking off a demerit in the quad, I was met by one of the cooks who was leaving the kitchen. He was throwing out some garbage behind the cafeteria. It was a warm day and I was looking exhausted. He asked if I would like some water and I said, "Absolutely." While sitting in the cafeteria and drinking, he told me there was a better way to work off demerits. I begged him to tell me about this alternative method. Apparently, instead of walking the quad, you could get assigned to the kitchen during your free time. This duty entailed washing metal trays and flatware, mopping the floors, and helping with food preparation. This is where I learned to be a master at peeling potatoes. I never had to walk the quad again and I gained five pounds because they fed you while you were there in the kitchen.

The weeks seemed to move on quickly. I tried not to make any more mistakes, but that was unrealistic. The only good thing about this was that other recruits made bigger mistakes than I did. There were some unique recruits in my class. One was named recruit Williams. He was taller than most of us; probably six feet four or five inches. He had no muscle tone, though. He was big and tall and a bit lanky, but seemed to have no common sense. He probably would have trouble putting batteries in a flashlight. He wasn't disciplined and something as simple as making his bed was a challenge to him. Because of this, our group was constantly being given demerits for his mistakes. The instructors would never punish him, but punish us for not motivating him properly. This became exhausting for the rest of us because we ultimately had to make his bed for him. He was told by the group to sleep on top of the covers so the bed would never be disturbed. We thought that would eliminate the problem. Instead, it created a much worse one because he now slept naked on top of the covers and his major issue was flatulence. His farting during the night smelled like rotten cabbage. It became clear that this was never going to be acceptable and he was warned on numerous occasions to put an extra cover over himself during the night. He advised us that it wouldn't work because the blankets were itchy. Due to this situation, we soon devised a motivational exercise for recruit Williams.

During our physical training exercises, there were always muscle pulls or bruising. When that happened, the instructors would take us aside and put what was called "Atomic Bomb" ointment on the affected area. It went on cool but turned into lava within a minute or so. It was so hot that just a small amount was all that was needed. This became the inspiration be-hind the exercise we were about to implement, which involved waiting until Recruit Williams went to sleep. He always slept on his back, with his legs spread apart and his junk hanging out. I'm sure by now you can see where this story is going. Hours before, we drew straws to see who would place the Atomic Bomb oint-ment in the appropriate area. It was my friend Bill Daniels who drew the short straw, which was only appropriate since his bed was right across the way from Williams. At 2:30 am, the room was eerily quiet, except for the staccato sounds of gas. It was at this point that the ointment was applied to the offensive area. Within a few minutes, the sounds of farting came to an abrupt halt and screams of pain ensued. The next thing we saw was Williams leaping out of bed, jumping up and down, patting his junk, and screaming, "I'm on fire!" He ran to the showers and that's where we witnessed the funniest sight we have ever seen. There he was, lying on the shower floor with the water streaming down onto his brightly colored balls.

The sounds of the whole section laughing soon brought Sergeant Evans, who was the duty officer, into the bathroom. He demanded, "What are all you numbnuts doing out of your racks and why is Williams lying on the fucking bathroom floor, holding his balls?" Of course, none of us wanted to own up to our motivation of Williams, but the distinctive odor of Atomic Bomb filled the air. Evans looked at us with a sheepish grin and said, "I guess Williams was motivated properly." That was the last time he slept naked and on top of his covers until we graduated. And, by the way, he learned quickly how to make his bed properly.

Another crazy-bastard recruit was named Roger Treadway. He was about five feet nine inches tall, with brown hair. He walked with a slight hunch and he had crazy eyes. You just knew by looking at him that something bad was about to happen. This lunatic's nick-name was "Flame Thrower." He got it by be-ing able to shoot fireballs out of his mouth. He would fill his mouth with lighter fluid, then spit it out while putting a match to it. When he would do this between two and three o'clock in the morning, it sometimes set off the smoke alarm, causing us to vacate the barracks. The last time he pulled that stunt, all the sprin-klers went off, saturating everything in the section with water. We gathered up as many of our personal belongings as we could and ran out into the street, wrapped in our blan-kets. Needless to say, that was the last time the "Flame Thrower" tried that stunt. He al-most got expelled from the academy and the only thing that kept him there was the fact that his father was personal friends with the commandant. Instead, Treadway received five demerits.

A crucial part of our training was weapon familiarity and, most of all, safety. Recruit Jay Rayburn failed to understand this policy. Rayburn was a slightly overweight black man with an inferiority complex that made him think everyone was picking on him because of his color. Of course, this had nothing to do with his race. It had everything to do with him just being plain stupid. He had no business being a potential police officer because he didn't abide by any of the rules and regulations. He thought they didn't apply to him. He was counseled many times and with all the demerits that he so often earned, he was rarely allowed to go home on weekends because he couldn't possibly work them all off in any given week.

The straw that broke the camel's back came early in the fourth week of training. The class was starting to weed out the deadwood. Our class had started with eighty-eight men and was already down to seventy. On this particular occasion, we were on the pistol range. The men who had already qualified were assisting a group who had not yet mastered their weapons. Rayburn was last in trying to qualify and was about to be dropped from the academy. Recruits were only given a certain number of chances to pass the course and if not completed in the given time frame, they would be released. Because Rayburn was so deficient in firearms, they wouldn't allow a classmate to tutor him. As a result, Instructor Taylor, one of the range officers, had to assist with his instruction. This would be Rayburn's last chance to qualify.

The qualifications were about to begin for the final time that day. Seven recruits needed to pass this last test. Six had accomplished their qualification; only Rayburn was left. We were all observing intently when things were abruptly halted. What happened was that Trooper Taylor had given Rayburn a specific set of instructions and said, "On the whistle, proceed in firing your weapon." Once the whistle blew, the next thing we saw was Rayburn unholstering his weapon and twirling the gun as if he were Wyatt Earp. As a result, the weapon fired backward, hitting the ground between Taylor's legs. At that point, the weapon was removed from Rayburn's hands and the instructor grabbed him by the throat, attempting to choke him. We all rushed over, thinking that the trooper was shot, but fortunately the bullet missed him. It was then our job to stop Taylor from killing Rayburn. Several of us jumped on our instructor, pulling his arms and hands away from the limp body of our classmate. He eventually gasped for air, sat up, and was informed by the other instructors that it was his last day and to go back and pack his gear. His time as a recruit and a potential police officer had officially ended.

Another classmate that needed to be "motivated" was recruit Teddy Ottinger. He was about six feet four and a half inches, with dark black, oily hair that was longer than academy regulation. No one seemed to understand why he wasn't given demerits for that. His weight was about two hundred seventy pounds, but not in a muscular way. He used to trash talk the smaller recruits about how he was going to punish them in the upcoming boxing schedule, which took place in the seventh week of training. He was a very intimidating person who appeared to be all talk. It seemed as if his group was constantly getting demerits for his inadequacies and flagrant violations of academy rules and regulations. For example, he had a disheveled appearance and always looked dirty. His uniform was constantly wrinkled, his tie always had food stains, and the buttons on his shirt were never buttoned correctly. He was the typical fuckup for which his classmates paid the price. This didn't sit very well with either his instructors or his roommates. It seemed that the people that screwed up the worst were never penalized directly. Instead, their classmates would pay a heavy price for not being able to motivate them properly. This was becoming very old, so it was decided that Ottinger would be taught a motivational lesson.

My friend, Big Joe Morris, was in a different

group from me. He stood about six feet six inches tall and weighed about two hundred and ten pounds. He had brown hair and brown eyes along with a great smile and dimples. You couldn't help but like this guy when you saw him. He ultimately became my lifelong friend. Recruit Ottinger was in his group and he was the primary cause of them receiving numerous demerits. As you recall, if you have demerits that aren't worked off, you don't go home. Many of these recruits had families that they desperately wanted to see. They couldn't take it any longer, so a plan was devised to teach Ottinger a valuable lesson.

Joe and representatives of his group approached me after dinner one night and asked if I would be willing to help motivate a particular recruit who was giving them all kinds of distress. Their plan was a simple one that would be carried out during Boxing Week. Ottinger was scheduled to box another recruit that was close to the same size as him. Ottinger was bragging about how he was going to take apart his opponent and that they wouldn't even go a full round. There was also talk that there was betting being done on this particular match. Joe asked me if I would agree to switch my scheduled match so I could be Ottinger's opponent. Because I was smaller in height and weight, we would need some inside help; namely, Sergeant Spencer, who was the boxing instructor. It had been explained to him that this was going to be motivational and a great lesson would be taught. Spencer knew that Ottinger was a fuckup and that the group had been receiving all of these demerits as a result of his lack of compliance with the rules and regulations, so he was happily onboard with changing the schedule.

When Ottinger found out that the schedule had been changed, he was smiling from ear to ear – mainly because there was going to be a drastic weight difference (about thirty-five pounds) between us. What he failed to realize was that I had fought nineteen amateur boxing matches before entering the police academy and had a record of 19-0. He had no idea that all hell was about to be unleashed on him. Then came the day of the actual match. There were six matches before our heavyweight match and all of the recruits stayed to watch the last matches of the day. Each match consisted of three two-minute rounds and a knockdown would not stop the match. The referee could give the downed boxer a standing eight count and he couldn't be saved by the bell. It was crystal clear that Sergeant Spencer wanted each recruit to box for the full six minutes.

Ottinger entered the ring wearing his academy shorts and t-shirt with a towel around his neck. He held his gloves above his head and, with a cocky smile, looked around the room. He thought this was going to be a punishing six minutes for his new opponent. As it would happen, he was in for a rude awakening. I entered the ring dressed the same way and was told to come to the center of the ring, where Spencer advised both of us about the rules of the match, then told us to return to our respective corners and wait for the bell. As it rang, Ottinger approached and swung his right fist wildly toward my head. Ducking under his attempted blow, I sent a right cross to the head, followed by a left to the stomach, causing a loud gasp and the loss of his mouthpiece. Normally, the fight would have been stopped to replace the mouthpiece, but Spencer said to continue. The remainder of the round was a brutal ass-kicking by me. Ottinger was down three times, looking for the sergeant to stop the fight. Spencer's answer was, "Get up, you big baby, and fight." The next two rounds were even worse than the first. He spent almost the entire last two rounds on his back, stomach, or knees, looking for anyone to stop this punishment. When the bell finally rang, ending the fight, he was carried to his corner and sat on his stool, bleeding profusely. Joe Morris quietly whispered in his ear, "You've been officially motivated. No more fuckups or this will be the beginning. Do you understand?" With his head hanging down, he nodded yes. That was the last time that group got a demerit because of Ottinger.

The week of graduation was probably one of the easiest weeks we had at the academy. The instructors called us by our first names and there was very little physical training. It was mostly just taking final exams and practicing graduation exercises. But there is one story that could have ended it all for my group.

The night before graduation, my group decided that we needed a party. The plans were simple. Recruit John McAvoy was working at the front gate from 9:00 to 11:00 pm. One of us would go and use the phone at the gate to order pizza for delivery (because leaving the grounds was a dismissible offense). We were also going to have the local tavern deliver us some beer. One of the guys had smuggled in some porno tapes, so all we had to do was borrow the projector from the classroom. We felt like we had been through hell for almost eight weeks and this was going to be our reward.

To ensure our secrecy and that we didn't get caught, we covered all the windows and doors with blankets so no light would penetrate the building, because "lights out" was at 10:30 pm. To our good fortune, the officer of the day was Sergeant Spencer. He treated us with respect and he was a "guys' guy." We knew his routine down to the minute. At 9:30 pm, he would start his inspections of the barracks. He would drive by in this old clunker of a jeep that you could hear coming from blocks away. If he saw any lights on, he would stop by the front door and simply say, "Go to sleep." Everything went like clockwork. Spencer made his pass in the jeep, gave his shout out, and moved on. What we didn't count on was him returning on foot at 11:00 pm to check on one of the recruits who had recently been ill. Spencer slipped in through the door behind us by moving the blanket aside. We were all facing the sheet, watching porn and eating pizza and drinking beer, so we didn't notice him enter our barracks. I felt a tap on my shoulder and a voice said, "Get me a slice and a cold one." Little did I know who was asking for the pizza and the beer; I assumed it was one of the guys. After passing the food and drink backward, out of the corner of my eye I noticed a bright yellow stripe down the side of a pant leg. I was speechless. I started to sweat and had a hard time breathing because I knew one day before graduation, we could all be expelled for breaking academy rules. As I sat in terror for the next few minutes, the voice whispered again. He said, "I like pepperoni." I called up front for a slice of pepperoni pizza to be passed back, then handed it over my shoulder and it disappeared. The next few minutes seemed like an eternity. When I finally mustered up enough nerve to turn around and explain, he was gone. He had quietly slipped out. I told the others to put on the lights and explained what had just happened. None of us slept well that night for fear of not graduating.

On graduation morning, we all dressed in our Class A uniforms and marched onto the parade grounds. We heard speeches from the commandant and various dignitaries. The class was summoned and, one by one, we received our graduation diplomas. When they called my name, I walked up, saluted the staff, and extended my hand while receiving my diploma. Sergeant Spencer smiled at me with a boyish grin and whispered in an ever-so-soft voice, "Next time, make it thin crust" and gave me a wink. I never forgot that. Over the next thirty-seven years, I had on occasion met up with Sergeant Spencer and we talked about that incident and laughed so hard that we had tears in our eyes. It was one of the best memories I carried with me throughout my academy days.

CHAPTER 3
FIRST ASSIGNMENT

Almost three months to the day after I graduated from the police academy, my journey was about to begin. Friendships that were forged would become a brotherhood. There was a dedication to each of my classmates that cannot be explained. Nowhere in the job world would you find a fellow worker so willing to put himself in harm's way or lay down his life for his brother. Little did I know then that this profession, over the next thirty-seven years, would bring me to my highest highs and my lowest lows. There would be tears of joy and tears of pain, both physically and, more importantly, psychologically. How could all these emotions be wrapped up in one profession?

I was advised by the scheduling sergeant that I was to report to "B-Squad." The squad was working the day shift from 8:00 am till 4:00 pm and my shift lieutenant was James Carr. He was a "good ole boy" from Mississippi. I think he was still fighting the Civil War and he didn't care much for a transplanted New Jersey boy. He would never speak to the troops; he would tell the squad sergeant what he wanted, even if you were standing right next to him. My squad sergeant was the poster boy for a Marine drill instructor. His name was William Morga. He was a stickler for rules and regulations and probably could recite them in his sleep, but felt they didn't apply to him. His appearance was all military: spit-polished shoes, leather shining, brass looking like mirrors, and the personality of a pit bull. His attitude was, "Do as I say and not as I do." He liked to drink and every other word out of his mouth was a curse or an insult. He was someone you didn't want to cross. In my eyes, he was a terrible role model as a supervisor. In all fairness to him, though, he taught me all the things not to do and, as a result, I became a better supervisor down the road. The problem I had with him was that he loved to ridicule you in front of the other officers. I think it made him feel good about himself. I would often think that if there ever came a time when I was a sergeant, I would never belittle my officers and make them feel embarrassed. I would want to offer them constructive criticism and take them aside to give them some positive reinforcement, leaving them with something encouraging that they could take with them.

Right after inspection, the new probation officers would be assigned a training officer. This officer was supposed to guide and evaluate your progress over the next two months. Much to my dismay, I was assigned to Officer Jimmy Noland. He was a ten-year veteran, but newly assigned to B-Squad. His attitude was, "Let someone else do it. Never volunteer and don't make waves." I truly wanted to learn, but this was never going to happen under his tutelage. My first day consisted of going for coffee for the lieutenant, picking up the newspaper, and sitting in the patrol car watching the nurses go to their cars at the hospital. This was not the police department my family told me about. This was not what I envisioned my professional career to be. For the next two weeks, that was my daily routine and I was beginning to doubt my choice of profession. Nordic Foods seemed a million miles away. I could still hear Peter Swenson's voice saying, "Are you sure this is what you want?"

After four tours on day shift, I was assigned a new training officer. His name was Officer Jake

Lane, but to the other officers, he was better known as "Ass Kicker." He only had four years on the job, but he had earned that nickname many times over. He wasn't a very big man, probably only standing about 5'9" and weighing one hundred fifty-five pounds, but if I had to go on a bar fight or a domestic call, there was no one better to have at your side. When he was in the Navy, I heard he was a Fleet boxing champion and there was nothing that I saw that would have indicated otherwise.

There was a time when we were given a warrant to serve and it was for an assault on a woman. I found out later that not only did this guy often beat up his wife, but he thought it would be funny to push his disabled step-daughter out of her wheelchair and watch her try and get back in. Jake told me about this as we entered the house. Needless to say, I was very upset with this information. He told me to go and speak to the wife and get as much information about the incident as I could. Seated in the living room, wearing just his underwear and slippers and drinking a forty-ounce bottle of beer, was the man for whom the warrant was issued. There was some talking and I could hear the man telling Jake to get the hell out of his house. I then heard a very loud crash and glass breaking. As I ran to the living room, there was Jake, calmly talking to a small girl and wiping the tears off of her face. She was seated in a wheelchair, but there was no sign of the man. Looking around the room, I asked, "Where did he go?" Jake said that he left. I replied, "What do you mean, he just left?" He pointed to the window and as I walked toward it, I could see that the blinds were all mangled and hanging straight down. I looked out into the backyard where the man was lying on his back with the warrant shoved in his mouth. Looking back at Jake, I said, "What the hell?" He just smiled and stated the man had tried to escape and resisted arrest. He told me to go outside and cuff him, then let headquarters know we had one under arrest and have the first aid stand by in the cell area. As the years went by and this story was told and re-told, I would be asked, "Is that how he got the name Ass Kicker?" Today, I would smile and say, "Oh, no...that just reinforced it."

When probation was over, there was a posting of permanent assignments. I couldn't wait for the day when I would be working by myself in my car. I received a call from my academy classmate, Big Joe Morris. He was working desk duty and was still on probation due to Division Captain Greg Hardy's evaluation that Joe was unfit for police work because he was color blind. The department doctor had cleared Joe months before, saying his color blindness would not affect his performance as a police officer, but Hardy kept him on probation anyway.

When I picked up the phone, I could hear Joe talking to another officer, saying, "Wait till I tell him where he's going." The next words I heard almost knocked me off my feet. It seemed I would not be getting my patrol car and squad assignment. Instead, I was being assigned to the Narcotics Undercover Unit. I said, "Are you fucking kidding me?" Joe said that he had the paperwork right there in his hand. I was to report to Sergeant LaRocca that Saturday at 8:00 pm. I looked into the phone and muttered, "Holy shit." I never expected this. It seemed LaRocca, who had the ear of the chief of the department, wanted me and requested that I be assigned to his unit.

On Saturday at 8:00 pm, I was standing in the office of the narcotics unit supervisor. As I looked around the room, I was pleasantly surprised to see Jake Lane, Bill Davis, Paul Kola, and Danny Conway. All of these guys were good cops and the type who would cover your back when needed. Sergeant LaRocca was very political. He used politics the way a skilled surgeon used a scalpel, knowing when to do favors and when to look the other way. His favorite expressions were, "Keep the wolves off my back" and "All the trouble is in the other room." We all learned very quickly what that meant.

That first year in narcotics was a true learning experience. I had worked with Jake Lane, a.k.a Ass Kicker, before so I pretty much knew where I stood with him. Bill Davis was the senior statesman of the unit. He stood about 5'10" with a slight potbelly. He had brown hair with a touch of gray, furrowed brows that always made him look intense, dark brown eyes that always looked as if they were looking through you rather than at you, and he was a good ten years older than all of us, but had a wealth of information and experience that went a long way. Danny Conway was a big kid, strong as a bull, and had the same mentality. He stood 6'5", weighed around two hundred and fifty pounds, with dark black hair, blue eyes, and quite a few tattoos from when he served in the Navy on submarines. He knew only one direction and one speed and that was straight and hard. When he had his mindset on going somewhere, you knew to just clear a path and get out of the way or there would be a very good chance you would be run over by the train. Now Paul Kola, he was the right-hand man of LaRocca. He had a dark complexion and weighed about two hundred and twenty pounds on a good day. He had a distinctive gut that always hung over his belt. When he walked, he had this swagger that made him almost appear like a Weeble. You may remember the old jingle, "Weebles wobble but they don't fall down." When he spoke, he had a very heavy Brooklyn accent. Whenever you saw LaRocca, Kola was almost always with him. I think it had something to do with both of them being Italian. There were three Irish guys and two Italians on this squad and I could see where their trust would lie.

There were occasions when we were assigned another officer, John Gurdak. He was our report writer. The paperwork at times was mountainous and he would come in with his typing skills and fly through reports. This ultimately allowed us more time in the field. He wanted desperately to do fieldwork and he was constantly hounding LaRocca to let him go into the field with the rest of the unit. This went on for months and was starting to get under LaRocca's skin. Every time Gurdak was assigned to us, this scenario played out. We could see it was starting to wear thin with LaRocca. Then came the day that we were working Vice.

There was a prostitution ring operating in the apartment areas and the complaints were piling up on the chief of detectives' desk, so we were given the word to clean it up ASAP. As usual, Gurdak was the first person in LaRocca's office, lobbying for a field assignment. But this day was going to be different. I guess LaRocca had enough and it was time to teach Gurdak a lesson.

We used to call Gurdak "The G Man." It made him feel like one of the boys. We all had nicknames. Mine was "Crash" and it was earned by my being able to take down a door with one shot, whether it was using my body or the sledgehammer. As you already know, Jake Lane was "Ass Kicker," and Bill Davis was "Gonzo," mainly because he was a little bit crazy. His idea of a good time was killing things, stemming from his days of serving in the Marines. During the Viet Nam War, Gonzo won two Purple Heart awards and a Bronze Star for valor. Paul Kola was "The Duke," named after the baseball player Duke Snider. He loved the Dodgers and he sounded like he lived in Brooklyn all his life. Danny Conway's nickname was "Kodiak," like the bear, with hands that were double the size of most others. He wore a size 15 shoe and you know what they say about shoe size. That could be the reason he was banned from every house of ill repute. They would see him coming and run out the back door. Gonzo had another nickname for him and it came from the time Gonzo served in the Marines in Viet Nam. He called him "Beaucoup." The spelling may be off, but it was loosely a Vietnamese/ French term for "fucking huge."

LaRocca called a meeting and advised us that the G-Man was going on this assignment and he was going to be the lead officer. Gurdak was ecstatic to finally be going out in the field. He would be acting as a John and we would be monitoring him with a wire that he would be wearing. Just before he was going undercover, we worked out the signs, both verbally and physically, so there would be no doubt when the bust would take place. He was told that as soon as the prostitutes gave him a price for services that constituted the violation, we would come in and make the arrest. If for any reason there might be a malfunction in the wire, all he had to do was pull up the shades and we would know the violation took place and we would burst through the door. LaRocca asked if everything was clear and he confirmed, "Crystal."

We followed Gurdak's car to the area where the women were working, gave a last-minute check on the wire, and all was working fine. Approaching his car were two very heavyset black women weighing nearly two hundred pounds each. One had her hair dyed blonde while the other had a kind of purplish tint. They were wearing something that resembled a "Mr. T" starter set and the tightest stretch pants I had ever seen. These women were extremely top-heavy and for the life of me, I couldn't imagine them ever making any money whatsoever. The conversation went something like this: "Hey sugar...what are you doing out this late in the neighborhood? Maybe you're looking for a good time." The G-Man's answer was not clear, mainly because he was sweating so badly he was shorting out the audio. Next, we heard, "Why don't you come to our apartment and we can have a threesome?" The laughing in the van was almost deafening. I'm not embarrassed to say that there was definite leakage. Jake was on the floor, tears were running down my face, and LaRocca said, "This should take care of him wanting to work in the fucking field unit forever. Make sure he's safe, but let this go as far as you can." The door opened on the G-Man's car and all three walked toward the apartment. The sight of him in the middle of these two women walking arm-in-arm was hilarious. Remember, he was only 5'5" at best, with shoes on, and weighing around one hundred and thirty-five pounds. Each of the women had him by at least five inches and fifty to sixty pounds. This was going to be a night we all would remember for our entire career. About twenty minutes later, we saw the blinds go up. The wire was transmitting poorly. I'm sure it was soaked by now from his profuse sweating. Jake asked, "What do you think? Should we go in?" I looked at LaRocca and he replied, "Give him a few more minutes." Then it happened. At the window was the G-Man. He was pulling so hard on the shades that they came off the window.

Rushing out of the van and hitting the door on a dead run, it crumbled like cardboard. As we entered the apartment, there on the floor was one of the most frightening scenes I had ever seen. As it turned out, it also became the absolute funniest sight that I have ever seen. Blankly staring up at the ceiling, wearing only black knee-high socks and the elastic from his torn underwear, lay the G-man. He was covered with some type of brownish-black substance. I initially suspected it was blood, but I was wrong. I thought at first that they had killed him when they found the wire, but somehow he convinced them it was a transistor radio. Unbelievable as it may seem, the women bought it. Then my eyes switched over to Jake, who was now sitting on the couch, laughing uncontrollably. I realized the dark brownish substance was not blood but chocolate syrup smeared all over his body, and next to that was a large can of whipped cream. Let's not forget the hookers. They were kneeling on either side of the G-Man. One was rubbing his chest while the other was rubbing between his legs, trying to arouse something that resembled a very tiny acorn. I'm sure his panic during the situation was directly responsible for his dick shriveling up into a tiny nut. It was a sight that would be branded on my brain forever. We got G-Man off the floor and I asked Jake, "Should we clean him up?" He said to just get Gurdak a sheet. Not wanting to get covered in chocolate syrup, I grabbed him by the ears and put him on the couch. We couldn't help but notice that he was mumbling something incoherently and blankly staring at the far wall.

LaRocca entered the apartment about ten minutes later, looked around, and just smiled. Then, sitting next to the G-Man, he said, "How did your first field assignment go? Wanna do another one?" Gurdak looked at him, then at us, and answered, "No, I think I'm good." From that point on, the G-Man just wanted to be known as Officer John Gurdak.

CHAPTER 4
THE NIGHT ELMER FUDD MET THE WEED

While I'm still reminiscing about stories of my days in the Narcotics Unit, this one will always bring a major smile to my face. Revenge can be so sweet. As my assignment was coming near an end, the squad started to become more mischievous, but not in a bad way. We were more like practical jokers trying to pass the time. There was the night that Joe Polk and I were out looking for our C.I. (Confidential Informant). Joe was temporarily assigned to the Narcotics Unit due to a shortage of manpower. He was a lifelong friend who came onto the department two academy classes after mine. We went to the same high school together and played on the same baseball team. He was about 5'10", one hundred and eighty pounds, with a full crop of blond hair and an unbelievable wit. He could make you laugh just by giving you a side look. We always seemed to be on the same page together, finishing each other's sentences. He was also a Navy veteran, having served in the submarine service.

We found our C.I. at the local bowling alley. When he saw us, he tried to hide something down his pants. Of course, we took him into the restroom, pulled off his pants, and found a bag of weed. His answer was, "I was just holding it for someone." Yeah, right. Joe told him, "You screw with us and you're on a one-way trip to the county jail" and that's the last place he wanted to go. There were some really bad boys waiting to get their hands on him; after all, he did help put them there. After some heart-to-heart conversation, he gave up the name of his weed man. We then sent him on his way, taking the bag of weed and throwing it in the back seat of the car. Usually, at the end of our tour, we would dump it down the toilet. At around 11:00 pm, we came back to headquarters and pulled behind the building, where the chief of detectives' office faced the rear. It was also on the ground level. Looking in his office, we could see Captain Hardy sitting in his chair, smoking his pipe.

Hardy was a burly man. He was about 6'

2" with salt-and-pepper-colored hair. He had a distinctive jaw that jutted out almost to a point. Even though he was Chief of Detectives, he always wore a uniform. Hardy also had a speech impediment that made him sound like Elmer Fudd. You could always tell when he was around by the smell of burning pipe tobacco. He was always having conversations with his men while smoking his pipe. The pipe would rise and fall with every word spoken and sparks from the burning tobacco would fly out, landing all over his shirt and tie. I guess that was why he preferred wearing a uniform rather than a jacket and tie.

On this particular night, all the signs were there for the perfect prank. Remember, because he sounded like Elmer Fudd, you couldn't have any conversation with him without thinking, "Where's that qwazy wabbit?" Most of all, he couldn't pronounce the letter C. That was bad, because his lieutenant's name was Cliff Johnson. When he called for him, it came out "Qwiffy." You would fall on your ass laughing just listening to him speak.

With Captain Hardy, the weather could be freezing outside, ten degrees with the wind howling and snowing like crazy, and he would still have the window open in his office. This was the perfect opportunity to get rid of the weed we had confiscated, which normally would have been flushed down the toilet. As Joe and I approached his window, Hardy had just left to go to the dispatch office. Reaching in, we took his pouch of Captain Black tobacco and filled it with the weed. We then went back to our car and waited. It wasn't long before he returned. He was so predictable that within minutes, he picked up his pipe and stuffed it with the "good stuff." I was laughing so hard, I'm pretty sure I wet my pants. Joe fell out of the car door and was sitting in the parking lot, crying from laughing hysterically. We kept watching and the captain kept smoking.

Then it happened. Hardy got up from his desk, went to the doorway, and called Lieutenant Johnson, "Qwiff, Qwiffy." Johnson answered, "Yes, sir. What can I do for you?" Hardy answered, "I got a real bad case of the munchies. What you got to eat?" Tears rolling down my face, I couldn't even speak. How could this get much better? It did. Johnson had no food in the building, so he called the local diner and told the sector car to make a pickup for the captain. He returned within a few minutes with a ham and cheese sandwich. Hardy took the food into his office, placing it on his desk, unwrapping the paper, and preparing to eat, but for some reason, he got up and went to the lieutenant's desk. With Hardy stepping away, the target of opportunity was staring in our face and yes, we took it.

Scrambling out of the car and racing toward the window, I reached in and ate half of the sandwich, leaving just the crust. Joe and I went back to the car and continued to watch. Hardy returned to his office, sat down, looked at the sandwich and then down at the floor and up at the ceiling. He got up, stepped into the doorway, and called, "Qwiffy." With no response from the lieutenant, he walked down the hallway. Again we struck. Reaching in through the window, we ate the other half of the sandwich, leaving just the crust before Hardy and Johnson returned to the office. They both looked at what was left of the ham and cheese sandwich. Hardy, shaking his head, said, "I can't believe it. I'm still hungry" and Johnson asked if he would like another sandwich to be ordered. The captain replied, "Naw... I'm trying to cut back. One sandwich is enough." Joe could never look at Hardy or watch an Elmer Fudd movie ever again without laughing uncontrollably. The next day, I told Big Joe about the prank and we also let him know he was avenged for the color blindness crap.

CHAPTER 5
THE DRUG DEALER AND THE TRAIN

The patrol officers were getting several complaints about drugs being sold around this one particular school. Jake hated dealers, but even more so, those that sold drugs to children. We were sitting at a stakeout when he turned to me and said he was going to ask the sarge to let him work this case and wanted to know if I wanted in. I told him it sounded good. The next morning, we were in LaRocca's office, asking for permission to go off-book and try to get these dealers away from the schools. The only restriction was "no beatings." LaRocca was getting a lot of heat from the high brass about people going to the hospital for what seemed to be "excessive force." Jake's answer was always, "They resisted arrest. You got to do what you got to do. Protect yourself." As we left the office, I looked Jake straight in the eye and asked, "How far do you think we can go with this?" He just looked back at me with that stupid grin, which only meant someone was going to get hurt. I shook my head and hoped he wouldn't kill anyone.

One week into the stakeout, we caught a break. One of the patrol guys picked up a stoner, whose name was Tommy Bedwell, and turned him over to Jake and me. The stoner was a local lowlife who was getting his supplies from a heavy hitter in Springfield. Bedwell was a low-level dealer who tried to make people believe that he was the main supplier when in fact he was just a local dirtbag. He was about six feet tall, a hundred and twenty pounds soaking wet, and always wore a pea cap backward on his head and a Grateful Dead t-shirt. He had made the mistake, years before, of breaking into a liquor store and coming face to face with the owner's one-hundred-and-forty-pound Rottweiler. Bedwell had scars on his legs, his ass, and the back of his neck from when he was attacked by the dog. He was always filthy dirty and hung around with a woman called Babe. She got that name from the kids in the area, who said she looked like the baseball player Babe Ruth.

We wanted the name of Bedwell's supplier

and we were going to get it one way or the other. Of course, Jake was his usual, understanding, law-abiding servant of the law. Sometimes he bent the law just a little and sometimes he bent it into a pretzel. During the Q and A, Jake kept referring to Mr. Bedwell as Mr. Bedwetter, which got the guy's panties in a crunch. Then came what I expected all along. Bedwell stood up and tried to leave by pushing Jake. What a mistake. In the blink of an eye, Tommy Boy's head was bouncing off the trunk of our car. I was trying to count the number of thuds, but they came too quickly. I looked at Jake and said, "Resisting arrest, and should the first aid stand by at headquarters?" His answer was, "Hell, no. We're not even close to that yet." I knew this was going to be a long night.

Jake turned to me and said, "Crash, open the trunk of the car." I thought, "Here we go; just what LaRocca said: 'No beatings' and that was gone a long time ago." My fear was how far Jake was willing to take this. He said to just drive and that he had a place where we could get some straight answers. As we neared the railroad yard, he told me, "Stop right here. We're going to chat a little." Out of the trunk came Bedwell. The look on his face was that of a man going to the electric chair. His head turned from side to side. Finally, he asked,

"Where the hell are we? This isn't headquarters." Jake went right up to his nose and they stood looking at one another for what seemed like an eternity. Then Jake demanded, "For the last time, where do you get your shit from? I want the name or you will not see tomorrow, understand?" Bedwell said, "If I tell you, he will kill me." Jake's response was quick. He grabbed Bedwell, dragging him by his shirt toward the railroad tracks, and threw him forward onto the ground. In one swift motion, Tommy Boy was handcuffed to the tracks. He was now sitting, straddling one of the tracks facing south. He declared, "I don't scare that easy. You two are cops and this would be murder."

There was a look on Jake's face that scared me more. He bent over and whispered in Bedwell's ear, "Murder? I don't think so, but maybe suicide. How does that grab you? Oh, one more thing – the 3:22 am will be along in ten minutes, so don't take too long to give me that name." Then he simply turned and walked away and sat next to me in the car. I was stunned and I remember asking, "You're not leaving him there, are you?" Jake replied, "Of course not. He'll give the guy up once he sees that train's light coming down the tracks." Sure enough, the 3:22 was right on time. I could see Bedwell pulling at the cuffs and looking toward the car. He kept yelling, "This has gone far enough! Take these fuckin' cuffs off!" Jake walked to the tracks and said, "Do we get the name or not?" The train was coming closer and you could feel the ground shaking. I was beginning to get a little nervous. That's when Bedwell finally said, "Alright! Alright, I'll tell you! Take these off!" Jake responded, "No, no. The name first, and it better be the right one. I know where you live." The next words out of Tommy's mouth were, "Santiago, Angelo Santiago. Come on, I gave you the name!" This better be the right one, I hoped for his sake, because I was pretty sure our next meeting with Mr. Bedwell would be worse if it wasn't.

Then came the best part. Jake turned to me and said, "Okay, take the cuffs off." I looked at him with a straight face and said, "Those are your cuffs. I don't have the key." Hearing this, Bedwell started screaming and crying. The train was now bearing down, with the horn sounding and the light flashing, when Jake at last said, "Oh, I'm sorry. Here is the key. It was in my pocket all the time." I took the key and uncuffed Tommy. As I looked at his pants, there was a huge wet spot in the front and a foul smell coming from the rear. Jake stated, "There is no way he is getting in my car smelling like shit. Put him back in the trunk." Before Jake closed the trunk, he looked at Tommy Boy's face and warned him, "One more thing. Any mention of this to anyone and you'll wish I didn't find that key. Understand?" There was just a simple nod before the trunk was closed.

Weeks later, with the cooperation of the state police, Angelo Santiago's narcotics business came to an end and the most amazing thing happened. The drug traffic in that school zone came to an abrupt end, too. Tommy Boy Bedwell and the Babe were arrested in South Carolina for selling narcotics to minors and served a long time in the South Carolina State Prison. I guess sometimes people never learn from their mistakes.

CHAPTER 6
ROBBERIES AND CAR CHASES

The winter of 1969 was uncommonly cold and there always seemed to be strong winds coupled with snow. It was the kind of cold that went right to the bone. I had put in my time in the Narcotics Unit and was looking forward to getting back on the road. The good news was that I had gotten reassigned to my old squad along with Jake Lane. There was a new shift sergeant; his name was Sal Alfano. The guys on the squad called him "Trooper" mainly because he always wanted to be a state trooper. He was too small and he had this trooper complex. If something wasn't done to his liking, he would always say, "The state police don't do it that way," but if something was done right, it was probably taught to you while at the state police academy.

He loved to tell stories to new officers about his exploits while he was on the job and how he singlehandedly caught two bank robbers. His version of this story was grossly exaggerated. Truth be told, the old-timers who worked with him gave a much different story. It seemed that Sal was on a coffee run for the shift commander when the call came in that the bank on the corner of Grove and White Oak had set off the silent alarm. All cars in the area were told to respond. As the patrol cars arrived on the scene, the bank personnel said the suspects had just left in a white, unmarked windowless van. While completing his coffee run, Sal turned onto Melrose Drive, where a white van fitting the description of the bank robbers, traveling at a high rate of speed, lost control and slammed into the rear of his car. Both the driver and passenger of the van were knocked out cold, as well as Sal. The pursuing patrol cars that came upon the accident scene dragged both of the unconscious robbers out of the van and handcuffed them. Sal had a laceration on his head that required six stitches, plus coffee burns in his groin from the hot coffee.

The top brass determined that if not for Officer Sal Alfano, the bank robbers might have gotten away. He received a departmental citation for his actions. I'm sure it helped that Sal's godfather was a generous contributor to the reelection of the mayor. He may not have always told things as they truly happened, but I think he believed in his own special way that they did. When Sal eventually was promoted to sergeant, his favorite story to tell the new officers, while pointing to the scar on his forehead, was how he received it while apprehending two armed bank robbers. His version was that without thinking of his safety, he blocked the road with his vehicle, causing the van to slam into the rear of his patrol car.

Sal was always a little nervous around Jake and me because of our rule-bending. I'm sure the narcotic stories that preceded our arrival on his squad didn't help with his ulcer. It was a few weeks before Christmas and the shift commander, Lieutenant Mike Donovan, wanted a special detail to patrol the shopping centers. There were numerous reports about cars being broken into, illegal parking, and shoplifting. He figured if he gave us this detail, it would limit the amount of trouble we could cause. As a result, Jake Lane and I were given the detail, along with a brand new patrol car that had only twenty miles on it along with that new car smell.

Receiving a new car was a monster coup for us because only the most senior officers were assigned new cars. Midway into the shift, over the county-wide radio band, we heard a broadcast of a high-speed pursuit coming from the next town over. The car being pursued by multiple police vehicles was heading into our town. We broke from the detail and positioned our car where we could see down County Highway 619. In the distance, red lights were approaching. The neighboring township was a small community with limited resources. Their cars were old and many should have been retired years before. The chatter coming across the radio was that the suspects were wanted for assault and armed robbery and were armed and considered dangerous. In the distance, we could see the suspects' car pulling away from the pursuing vehicles. As the car passed us, we pulled onto the highway and started to follow.

The pursuing cars could no longer maintain the chase. The suspects' car was no match for our new car with the monster engine. We closed the gap quickly and kept radioing the mile markers and cross streets. The speeds of both cars were by now in triple digits, but there was smoke coming from their car and it appeared that they blew an engine. They started to slow down. We knew that two miles up ahead was a traffic circle and at their rate of speed, they weren't going to make it. We slowed down on our speed and waited. As predicted, they hit the circle, lost control of the vehicle, and began to flip over several times. The doors flew open and three people were ejected, but the driver was still belted in his seat. We pulled onto the grassy medium and started checking on the bodies that were ejected. Two were dead at the scene and the third one had severed an artery in his leg. Before I could administer first aid, he bled out.

I started putting yellow blankets over the three lying on the grass. As I glanced over at the suspects' car, I noticed another yellow blanket being placed over the driver. I remember thinking, "What a waste of four young lives." We later found out the ages of the four suspects. The oldest was eighteen years old and the youngest was fifteen. Three of them were brothers and one was a cousin.

Sergeant Alfano arrived on the scene and his first question was, "Is the patrol car damaged?" I just looked at him, shook my head, and walked away. Here was a family getting ready for Christmas and who was going to tell them that their three sons and nephew were dead? The worst part about this senseless story was that the suspects only netted a total of $35 and the weapon they used was a toy gun. Although the Christmas season is supposed to be a happy time, it was about to get worse for me.

CHAPTER 7
THE HOUSE FIRE

Growing up in a large family during the holidays was extremely joyous, especially Christmas. We all looked forward to this time of year because we were together with all of the aunts and uncles, cousins, my grandparents, and my parents. Each year, as my father and I walked to where they were selling the Christmas trees, I would get more and more excited. I could smell the pine scent as well as the aroma of wood burning, mainly to keep the men warm as they worked at selling trees. Soon we would get to the best part: the tradition of picking out the perfect tree and bargaining for the right price. My dad was a master at it. There would also be hot chocolate in paper cups to drink and to keep your hands warm on a cold winter night. These were the memories I had as a child and I loved Christmas... until December 24, 1969.

It was a week before Christmas Eve and I was working the day shift when I received a call to respond to a complaint about a group of kids throwing snowballs at passing cars. I went to the home of Andrew Seever, the name that was given to me as one of the boys involved. After having a discussion with his parents, Andrew and I stepped out of the house and sat in my patrol car. I spoke with him about the dangers of throwing snowballs at passing cars. We talked about when I was a kid, like him, and got into some trouble doing the same thing, only my snowball went through the driver's side window and injured the man driving. Andrew seemed to understand the dangers of doing this and promised to never do it again. He was 12 years old.

It was a week later, on December 24, and the weather that night was extremely cold, hovering around zero degrees. I had just gotten a new winter uniform coat. It had a heavy liner and a fur collar. I could pull the collar up around my ears and it was as warm as toast. With my fur-lined gloves, I said to myself, "Old Man Winter, give me your best shot." We were working the graveyard shift, midnight till 8:00

am. I had just met with Big Joe Morris. He had brought me a large cup of coffee and it was about 2:30 am when the call came in for a house fire. The coffee got dumped and we took off toward the house. From a distance, I could see the sky and it was bright orange. This was a working fire. As my car came to a stop in front of the house, I recognized the name on the mailbox: Seevers.

Joe and I were first to arrive on scene and because of our proximity, we got there before the fire department. As I approached the front door, the flames were coming out of the up-stairs windows. Joe had gotten a ladder from a neighbor's house and was trying to put it up to the second-floor window. I kicked in the front door and the heat hit me like a blast furnace, pushing me backward a few feet. I could see into the living room and there were no flames there yet, but the heat was intense. I remem-bered from my training that fire is not the chief cause of death, but superheated air is. Instincts and training took over and I hit the floor, knowing that the air and heat would be more manageable at that level. As I crawled across the floor, I kept calling Andrew's name. Down the hallway, I crawled along touching the doors to see if they were hot. As I came to the second one, I could hear a faint cry.

Pushing the door in, I found the three children in a corner. Andrew was shielding his young brother and sister, ages two and four. Andrew's breathing was shallow but he was conscious. The younger children were not breathing. I couldn't possibly carry all three and I had to make a choice. I told Andrew to stay there and I would come back for him. I picked up the two younger children, knowing the smoke and air above me could be fatal, but there was no time to crawl; they weren't breathing. I took a deep breath, stood up, and ran toward the front door. In the heat and smoke, my eyes were watering so badly that I couldn't find the door. While running, I could feel the heat taking over me, but I knew I had to make it out. If I could just see the red lights of the patrol car, we could escape. I could hear Big Joe's voice and ran toward it. The screen door had somehow closed and the next thing I remember, I was hitting it and knocking it off the hinges. We were finally outside.

Joe took the children and gave them to some first aid members. Staggering on my feet, I remembered Andrew. As I turned to go back into the house, Joe grabbed me and said, "It's too late. There's no one left to save. You'll kill yourself." He was wrong. There was one more. I had made a promise that I was going back. Once more, I was on the floor. This time the heat was unbearable. My new winter coat kept the flames off my back, but my legs were burning. As I reached the door where I told Andrew to stay, I felt the doorknob was red hot. Using my glove, I pushed the door open and called his name, but there was no answer. I slid across the floor and found him. There was no time to wonder if he was alright. I picked him up and ran as fast as I could, hitting that same front door, and we flew onto the front lawn. There were people all around with oxygen bottles and blankets. As I was lying on my back, looking up at the sky, I started to realize that Christmas was never going to mean the same thing to me again.

I was taken by ambulance to the hospital because they needed to check my burns and see if there was any damage to my lungs. I was kept overnight while my hands and legs were treated for burns, and I was given some pain medication. The next morning when I woke up, I heard some nurses talking about the tragedy that happened the previous night and what a terrible Christmas this was going to be for that family.

I realized then that my efforts to save them were in vain. I couldn't imagine losing my whole family: mother, father, and three young children. I closed my eyes, wiped away the tears, and said goodbye to Andrew. I could only hope that he knew I kept my promise, and that I came back for him.

CHAPTER 8
THE SCHOOL BUS AND JENNIFER

I had hoped 1970 would be better, but I was wrong again. The nightmares of the Christmas fire were still fresh in my mind and sleeping at night was difficult. There were nights that I didn't sleep at all. It seemed like a bad dream from which I couldn't awaken. The smell of wood burning or a child crying would set off feelings of despair and helplessness. I needed to speak to someone, but who could I turn to? My pride kept me from being able to let out my frustrations. I was afraid the other officers would think less of me if I went crying to them. We are supposed to be able to handle any situation, show no emotion, and just get on with the business at hand. Nothing taught at the academy could possibly prepare you for something like this. How was this possible? Would I be able to endure 25 years of this? Only time would tell.

Just three weeks later, I would be tested again, only this incident would stay with me for the rest of my life. I was returning from the county court and it was a beautiful afternoon. The sky was clear and there was still some snow on the ground. The Christmas holidays were over, the kids were back in school, and I had plans to go to my family's house for dinner when I heard the call for a pedestrian hit by a bus. The sector car gave his location but he was a distance away. I, on the other hand, was just two blocks away. I picked up my radio mic and reported, "535 to headquarters...I'm responding...E.T.A. one minute."

Pulling up to the location, I noticed a group of people around a school bus. Looking down at the ground, I saw a small child lying near the rear tire. There was blood everywhere. It seemed that the school bus driver, while backing up, didn't see a group of children walking behind the bus. Three children were struck, with two being thrown to the side. The third, Jennifer McCauley, was struck and fell straight down. The bus driver never knew he hit the children and kept backing up. While doing so, he ran over the child's head, killing her instantly. I knelt next to her, took her head, and tried to hold it together. I remember sitting in the street cradling her, refusing to let her go. The first aid members kept telling me it was alright and to release her to them, but I couldn't. I thought if I let her go, she would die and I couldn't lose another child. I carried her into the ambulance, placing her on the gurney, and only then did I step back. I watched as the ambulance drove away, lights and sirens on, but I knew I had lost my fourth child in three weeks.

I needed some time off. I made an appointment to see the department doctor and he recommended to the division commander that I be given a week off. He wanted to see me every day during that time. I returned to work after that week was over, but there was still an emptiness inside me that I could not shake. I felt that I could no longer look past the present because at any time, anything could happen. Everything could be taken away from me at any moment.

I realized that time is precious and you should live for the moment. You never know when all that you have and love will be taken away from you. I wouldn't speak of this incident again until almost twenty years later. I now believe those three weeks were the start of my PTSD.

CHAPTER 9
MY FIRST BABY DELIVERY

Somewhere it's written that time heals all wounds. I suppose that's true, but how much time would have to pass to heal the mental wounds I was carrying around with me? On almost every call, I kept looking for that glimmer of hope to show me that things would get better. On Valentine's Day, while working the day shift, that glimmer turned into a magnificent sunrise.

I was dispatched on a first aid call for a woman with stomach pains. When I arrived, I was met by a woman in her late forties wearing a bathrobe. She looked much older than she said. I thought to myself for a moment that she must have had a hard life. When asked if she was the one with the stomach pains, she answered, "No, it's my daughter. I think it's her appendix." Her daughter was in the rear bedroom, lying on her side with her legs pulled up toward her stomach. I asked her to roll onto her back so I could evaluate her condition. As she did, much to my surprise, it became obvious that the cause of her pain was not her appendix. She was very pregnant and about to deliver. I called her mother into the room, pointed to her daughter's condition, and informed her, "Your daughter is about to have a baby. What's her doctor's name?" The shocked expression on the mother's face was all I needed to see. She responded, "Oh, my God. We thought she was just getting fat."

I went to the house phone, called headquarters, and told them to send the first aid squad at once because I had a pregnant woman who was going to deliver within minutes. Returning to the girl, I could see the baby was already coming and I was on my own. Flying through my head were lessons I had learned at the police academy about dealing with childbirth. At that point, training took over and I realized I was going to deliver a baby. Pulling off the blanket, I could see the girl's water had broken and contractions had started. With each contraction, she was becoming extremely nervous and was in a great deal of pain. I called to her mother, but she had gone to a neighbor's house for help. I was really on my own.

My hope was that this baby would not be a breech birth, where the child comes out feet first. To my good fortune, I did have some divine help. I guess God felt that I needed a break and the baby was coming out normally. Within seconds, there was another contraction and the baby's head was completely visible. After a second contraction and push, the shoulders appeared. Holding a towel in my hand, I prepared myself to receive the rest of the child. As she emerged, she was covered in a slippery mess of what appeared to me as an indescribable substance. And her color was kind of bluish, which scared the hell out of me. Holding the baby in my hands, I rolled her onto her stomach, cleared her small mouth, and hoped for the best. Then came the sound of the most fabulous cry I ever heard.

I wrapped the baby girl in a clean towel and when I turned around, there were two first aid members standing there. I couldn't tell you how long they were there watching us, because I was quite busy, but the taller of the two said, "Looks like you didn't need us." I leaned over and gave the new mom a kiss on the forehead and told her, "You did just great.

Congratulations. She's beautiful." Later that day, I checked on their condition with the hospital and was informed that the baby – Denise Mary Slayton, weighing 6 pounds, 8 ounces – was doing great and so was her mom.

I guess that biblical verse is true. In Ecclesiastes, there is something written that says, "There is a time for all seasons...a time to be born and a time to die." This had been more than bringing a new life into the world. It was the start of a healing process that would carry me throughout my career and my life. I delivered two babies while on the job, but Denise Mary Slayton showed me that with great heartbreak also comes unbridled joy.

CHAPTER 10
THE FERAL ANIMALS

I'm very proud of the fact that after 37 years, I only had one complaint signed against me. Now, on the other hand, any call dealing with animals led me on a direct line to either the division commander or the chief's office. I will attempt to tell my side of the stories in the following incidents. This way, you can make your own decision as to whether discipline was warranted.

During the summer months, we had an over-abundance of feral animals roaming the new developments near wooded areas throughout the town. The chief at that time was a man named Roger Perlew. He was tall and slender and only weighed about 135 pounds. His head was bald with the exception of a little bit of side hair, which he kept very short. He always had a small unlit butt of a cigar jammed in the corner of his mouth. No one knew what color his eyes were because he was always squinting. He was old school, but trying to be more progressive. That was actually kind of an oxymoron; like a jumbo shrimp, it just didn't make sense, but in his defense, he tried to do the right thing.

Sergeant Alfano called me into his office one day and asked if I wanted to work a special detail for the chief. If the Big Boss asked for a favor, it really wasn't a favor; you were going to do it no matter what it was, so of course I said it would be an honor to help out the boss. Alfano just smiled and said, "Report to his office 8:00 am tomorrow and don't be a wise ass."

The next morning, there I was: standing tall at 7:45 am and waiting for the man, Chief Perlew. To my surprise, Joe Polk was also there. I had known Joe since high school, but we had never worked together. He was not a very big man, standing about 5'10". He had piercing blue eyes and a smile that could make anyone laugh. He also had a biting wit. I had come on the job a year ahead of him. That day, we just looked at each other, wondering what the special detail was all about.

At 8:00 am on the dot, the boss arrived. He was a no-nonsense boss; he gave instructions once and expected you to follow them to the letter. On his desk, I noticed a long box. He kept tapping his fingers on it and saying, "This is your new job. Don't screw it up." Still never telling us what the hell the detail was, but we just kept nodding and replying, "Yes, sir." He rambled on for twenty minutes about feral dogs and how we had to humanely remove them from houses, schools, and public grounds because they were a safety threat to residents and children. We needed to transport them back to the animal shelter. He looked at us both and said, "Pick up that box, go out there, and take care of this problem. Any questions?" Before either of us could say a word, he pointed to the door and added, "Good. I'll be checking on your progress."

I picked up the box and Joe and I walked out to our assigned vehicle. It was a Chevy Suburban that had seen better days. It should have been scrapped five years earlier, because it really was a piece of junk. We should have known then that this assignment was not one that we were going to enjoy. We opened the rear doors, put the box on the floor, and opened it. For the first time, we realized what the special detail was. In the box was a tranquilizer rifle. We looked at one another with utter confusion before Joe commented, "I hope there are instructions." To our surprise, we found the written but extremely vague directions. The first thing noted, in capital letters, was that the dosage was CRITICAL and that overdosage could prove to be FATAL. The next thing stated was that the dosage was administered by weight. We saw several problems with this. Number one, there was only a dosage chart based on small, medium, large, and extra-large animals. Number two, they didn't give us any weight ranges for different sized animals. My suggestion to Joe was to just go out and estimate the weight. We would have to see for ourselves just what "critical dosage" meant. We found this out very fast.

After one week, I'm sorry to say that not one dog survived. I guess they weren't kidding when they said that dosage was critical and could be fatal. Of course, we were called into the chief's office for our progress report. Needless to say, the boss was not happy. After a half hour of ass chewing, his words of wisdom were to go out there and do it right. By the second week, we started using smaller dosages so as to not kill the animals. However, we learned a very valuable lesson. If you underdose an animal, all you accomplish is to piss them off and they will attack you.

On one occasion, we responded to an animal that appeared to be part beagle and God only knows what the other part was. While I was in the driver's side of the truck, Joe stepped out to get a clearer shot and administered the dosage. As the dart hit the dog, it immediately fell onto its side. Thinking this was okay, Joe started walking toward it. The dog jumped up and looked around with a crazy look in his eyes. The mouth was foaming with saliva. The next thing we saw, it was racing toward Joe and chasing him up onto the hood of our truck. This prompted him to administer another dose, trying to calm the dog down. Unfortunately, all that managed to accomplish was killing the dog from the second shot. As a result, we learned lesson number two: there would be no more underdosing.

After two trips to the chief's office about dog bodies piling up at the kennel, we were advised there had been numerous calls from the American Society for the Prevention of Cruelty to Animals, also known as the ASPCA, about poor treatment of our feral friends. We felt that, had we been given proper training on the use of the weapon and how to determine weight and dosage, our results may have been more successful.

Then came the last day of the special assignment. While we were out on doggie patrol, the sector car received a call that a very large dog was chasing some children by one of the elementary schools. The sector car responded by asking if the Special Dog Unit was in the area. As bad luck would have it, we were. We responded that SDU 611 was in the area and en route. Joe told me that it was a big dog and that he wasn't getting out of our truck. He said if I wanted the dog, I would have to do it. We switched seats and he drove while I got the tranquilizer gun ready. Arriving in the area, we were directed to the houses near Belmont School, where the dog was last seen. A neighbor came out and pointed to the rear of her neighbor's house, advising us that the dog was in that backyard but didn't belong there.

This particular yard backed right up to Belmont School and the children were outside playing. As I was about to get out of the truck, I saw him. This was indeed a very large dog. It was a Great Dane mix, but he appeared to be the size of a half dog and half bear. He had his two front paws on the fence, looking over at the kids playing. Standing on his back legs, he was over six feet tall. Joe glanced at me and said, "Go ahead. He's all yours." Perusing through the directions again, I was trying to figure out the correct dosage. He was obviously someone's pet, but he was barking and attempting to get over the chain link fence, which would jeopardize the children's safety, so I couldn't take a chance. While still in our vehicle, I whistled to the dog. He jumped the fence and ran toward me, barking and growling as if I was going to be his next meal. Joe laughed at me and said, "Shoot him." I had to quickly determine the dog's weight. Still remembering the beagle incident, I was not about to underdose him. I estimated him to be about 200 pounds.

The rifle was now loaded with the dosage for a 200-pound dog, but it was difficult to get a clean shot from inside the truck because he was running back and forth along the fence line, chasing after the children. Because I wasn't going to get out of the truck, I had to make a split decision to shoot the tranquilizer dart. The dart was a cylinder about the size of your thumb, with a bright red feathered tail and a needle point. As I was lining up the shot and squeezing the trigger, Joe's foot slipped off the brake, causing the truck to lurch forward at the exact same time the dart was fired. To my horror, I could see the dart go over a garage roof, red feather flying in the breeze. My next thought was, "Dear God, please don't let that dart strike a child." There were no 200-pound children in the school playground and I knew very well how the dosage was critical. If it wound up in a child, there would most definitely be a fatality.

Joe and I looked at each other and jumped out of the truck, running toward the backyard with our night sticks in hand. To our surprise, we turned the corner of the house expecting to see this monster of a dog, but we found nothing. He had jumped the opposite side of the fence and went into the wooded area next to the school. Discovering no children injured, our next duty was to find that dart because it still had tranquilizer in it for a 200-pound dog. Searching all over the yard, I could not locate it. That's when I heard Joe from about twenty feet away, calling out, "I found the dart and you're really not going to like this." I wondered how I could I not like this if we had located the dart. Walking toward Joe, I noticed he had this stupid shit-eating grin and was pointing to a spot just below his feet. The closer I got, the louder he laughed. He finally said, "I got a bad feeling we're going to the chief's office again." Looking down to where Joe was pointing, I saw where the dart landed. Holy crap. It was sticking out of a cat, and not a 200-pound cat. Bending over, I pulled out the dart. This poor cat couldn't have been any more than five pounds and I had hit him with a load made for an enormous dog. Oh yes...we were going to see The Man, for sure.

Less than an hour later, we were standing tall in front of The Man. On his desk was a shoe box and seated to the right of him was a woman holding some tissues to her eyes. Oh no, I thought. The chief looked straight at me, pointing to the shoe box, and demanded, "What do you think is in this shoe box?" I couldn't resist and replied, "Shoes?" His face turned a color of red I had never seen before. He then stood up, glared at Joe and me, and stated, "Your detail is over and the two of you will pay for this lady's cat. It will cost you each $50. Do you have a problem with that?" Before we could answer, he stared at us and said, "I didn't think so." As we exited the office, Joe shook his head, looked at me, and commented, "That must have been a cat made of gold. That's a third of our weekly pay. Next time, let's let Cujo eat him." Just for the record, the Golden Cat's name was Fluffy.

I always had a problem putting down any sick

animal, but I realized it was the humane thing to do and would never want to see an animal suffer. I was telling this to the other sector car one afternoon when I was dispatched to a sick animal call. The resident had asked if a patrol officer could come to the house and help put down the sick animal. The guy in the other sector car was Officer John Steiner, whose nickname was "C.J." – short for "Crazy John." This was because you never knew what was going to come out of his mouth. He had more stories than all of the Brothers Grimm combined, and they were all just about as believable. On the good side, he would do anything for you. If you needed a shirt, he would take it off his back and give it to you. Of course, he might also tell you that he took it off a Viet Cong general while fighting in the Delta, which is where he supposedly won his two Silver Stars and a Purple Heart. On a good day, he would tell you that he earned the Congressional Medal of Honor, but that's another story.

On this day, he was going to show me the proper and most humane way to put down a sick animal. We were to respond to 677 Hawkins Lane, where the animal was in the backyard, near the doghouse. Now, Hawkins Lane was a very old road. Most of the houses didn't even have numbers on them and you had to go by the names on the mailbox or by the description of the house. There were about twenty homes on that road and a good portion of the residents were related with the same last name, Haskell. We advised dispatch that we were having a difficult time finding the correct house. Their response was, "Knock on some doors," so we split the street. As I was speaking to one of the many Haskells, C.J. shouted, "I got it! Over here." I watched as he went into the backyard. As I reached the fence, I could see him bending over and talking to a dog in a doghouse. The next sound I heard was a loud bang. C.J. turned and walked away from the animal, telling me to get a disposable blanket out of my trunk and bring it to the backyard.

As I was returning to the fence, I heard the neighbor in the next yard over say, "Officer, I'm the one who called. The dog is over here." While I was processing this, I heard another voice exclaim, "Oh, my God! What have you done? You've killed my dog!" C.J. had shot the wrong dog. The next I saw of C.J., his car was driving down the street in a hurry. I went over and spoke to the original caller, informing her that a terrible mistake had been made and that another officer would be back as soon as possible. As I left the scene, I received a radio call advising me to return to headquarters immediately. I knew right then and there that a shit storm was about to happen.

I pulled over to the side of the road, reached into my back pocket, and took out my wallet to check and see if I had enough money to replace the dog that C.J. had killed. When I arrived back at headquarters, the shift commander advised me that The Man would like to see me at once. Heading down the hallway toward his office, I wondered, "How much money will this cost me and how much time off will I get?" As I reached the office door, the secretary told me to take a seat and that the chief would be with me in a moment. From his office, I could hear some yelling mixed with a whole lot of cursing, then a deadly silence. I knew I was next. The door opened and C.J. walked out. He looked at me and apologized, "Sorry. This was my fault and he knows the whole story. He doesn't want to see you and said for me to just take you with me." I was shocked and thrilled that I didn't have to stand tall in front of the chief yet again. C.J. took the heat for me. We decided to pick up some coffee and go back to our sector. From that day on, I never teased C.J. about his tall tales. He could have thrown me under the bus, but he didn't. We became very good friends and that friendship lasted for forty-five years. He passed away in 2011 and I still miss him. But his stories will last forever.

On the brighter side of animal stories, this one didn't cost me any money, but I did get a tremendous amount of laughs from it. Every time I heard a call where animals were involved, I would just cringe. Nearing the end of a 4:00 pm to 12:00 am shift, both sector cars received a call about two dogs running loose in the area of South Pine Street near the water plant. That night, we had Sergeant LaRocca as shift supervisor. He called me, Bill Davis, and Joe Polk to meet with him at the water plant. When we arrived, he told us that he had spoken with Councilwoman Janice Salta, who lived on South Pine Street. She was irate that we were not controlling the feral dog problem in her area. This brought back some really bad memories for me; I sensed money and time off coming just around the corner. LaRocca wanted her off his back, so his plan was to hunt these wild dogs down and dispose of them. He made it perfectly clear that "disposed of" meant killed. My first thought was that the last time we disposed of something, it cost me $50 and two days off. He said he had spoken to the chief and there would be no problem due to Ms. Salta being involved.

We devoted the next hour to finding the feral dogs. Around 11:00 pm, there was a call that two dogs were seen in the backyard of 27 South Pine Street. LaRocca advised us to respond and take care of the problem. Bill Davis was the senior officer and his plan was to enter the yard and see if the dogs were there. We parked our cars at the water plant and approached the house. We could hear dogs barking, so we knew they were still in the yard. Peering over a fence, we saw a large oval above-ground pool, a tool shed, and some patio furniture. We devised a plan for Polk and me to move to the right, around the pool, and flush the dogs toward Davis, who would "dispose" of them. It sounded like the perfect plan, but sometimes things just don't quite go as planned.

We started our move to the right and Davis went left, carrying his shotgun. The dogs were barking at us and they were large animals. With our flashlights shining on them, they ran toward Davis. To his surprise, they came out of the darkness in full stride, teeth bared and snarling, looking hell-bent on ripping him to shreds. The next sound we heard was a blast from his shotgun, followed by a tremendous rush of water. You guessed it; the shot hit the side of the pool, opening a gaping hole and causing water to pour out. The two dogs were swept away toward the basement windows. This all happened in a matter of seconds and Polk and I just stood there with our mouths open.

In the next moment, we started to laugh. As our flashlights hit Davis' face, his expression was absolutely priceless. Then reality set in. Let's do the math: one cat, $50; one dog, $50; and now how much was a very large pool and water damage going to cost? "Oh, my God," I thought. I'd be working my entire career for free, if I didn't get fired. As we looked around, to our disbelief, there were no lights coming on in the adjacent houses. Could they have slept through all this noise? All three of us very calmly turned and exited the yard, got into our cars, and drove away. Sitting in a gas station just down the street, I waited for what I felt would surely be the inevitable call, ordering us to return to headquarters or at least a meeting with LaRocca. To my utter amazement, no such call ever came and the shift ended without incident. I headed home, still fully expecting a phone call, but still none came. At 3:30 pm, I returned to headquarters for the start of my next shift. I caught up to Polk in the locker room and asked if he had gotten any calls, but he hadn't. How was this possible? Then he came up with this gem of a scenario: What if the resident was sleeping in the basement and 80,000 gallons of water came through the windows, along with two rabid dogs, and they all drowned or the dogs ate the resident? "Shut up," I told him. "When the shift starts, I'm going back to the house to see just what's going on."

When the sectors were being assigned, I asked LaRocca for that area again. "Why?" he asked. "You were just there last night." I told him I realized that, but wanted to see if those dogs we had lost came back because we didn't want Ms. Salta complaining. He consented, "Okay, but don't get into anything with her, understand?" When I arrived back at the house, all seemed normal from the front, but the backyard looked like a bomb went off because the pool was flattened, the windows in the basement were shattered, and there was vinyl siding hanging off the side of the house. In addition, there was lawn furniture scattered everywhere.

As I tentatively knocked on the front door, the neighbor next door called out, "Officer, can I help you? Those people moved out last month." Could my luck really be this good? Then the neighbor made me smile when she commented, "I was just about to call the owner because I noticed the pool must have given way and all the water was gone." I paused and said, "What a terrible shame." Then she inquired why I was here. Thinking quickly, I told her, "Councilwoman Salta wanted to make sure the neighborhood wasn't being bothered by feral dogs." What a silver-tongued devil I thought I was. The neighbor thanked me for my concern and I left. I met with Polk and told him all was good, then inquired about Davis. He had put in for a sick day. After being charged by the dogs and unexpectedly "shooting pool" the night before, he seemed to have caught a bad case of the Blue Flu, which is when a personal day is needed.

CHAPTER 11
LEROY BLEVENS

Roy, as we called him, was a street kid, with a whole lot of mouth and a very intimidating size. For years, it seemed he would push his way around the streets, threatening those who were smaller and more timid. His attitude was, "If I like it, it is mine." I originally knew Leroy Blevens from my younger days, when we were teenagers. We lived in the same neighborhood and I was about five or six years older than him. Even then, I knew he was going to be trouble. He was a big bully.

Roy was of German and Polish descent and was the middle of three sons. His father was very demanding and liked to punish his sons for the smallest infractions. He was a nasty drunk who worked for a trucking company as a laborer, then would drink at the bar for hours afterward. When he returned home from the bar, he would take out his frustrations on his family, which included his wife and all three sons.

Roy was now almost twenty years old and stood about six foot six, weighing about 280 pounds. His shoe size was 16 and he always wore construction boots that were never laced. He was imposing to look at, yet not in the greatest shape due to his fondness for drinking. He had dirty brown hair that covered his ears and was always unshaven. His face carried the scars of many run-ins with older men and his father. He had a noticeable scar running from the corner of his left eye to partially down his cheek. This was a gift given to him by an ex-girlfriend who struck him with a beer bottle when he was about 16 years old. The story goes that she was pregnant and asked him how he was going to handle being a father. His answer was, "Are you sure it's mine?" That is what prompted the beer bottle to the face. He also had a chipped front tooth that probably came from another of the many battles he was in over the years.

Let's talk about the night that Leroy Blevens saw the error of his ways. Our town had been notified by a neighboring city earlier in the evening that Roy was involved in an altercation at one of their bars and sent two men to the local hospital. By the time one of their cars got to the bar, he was gone. We were asked to keep an eye out for him because complaints were pending.

I was working in sector two, an area that had a lot of bars and liquor stores. That night, I was the only car working in that area due to a shortage of manpower. This was one of the department's biggest complaints – not enough officers. Jefferson Township was growing at a staggering pace and manpower-wise, we were not keeping up with the growth. At 10:30 pm, a call came in from one of the many bars on Augusta Street. The caller stated that there was an unruly patron who was refusing to leave and fighting with other patrons. I arrived at the bar within minutes and could see through the front window that a very large man was pushing the bar owner around. The man had his back to the front door and wouldn't let other patrons leave. As a result, they started exiting through the back door as quickly as they could. As I entered the bar, the man – who I knew as Leroy Blevens – looked at me and said, "Look here, one of the three little pigs has arrived. If you know what's good for you,

you'll get the fuck out of here right now, before I kick your ass."

It was quite obvious that Roy had been drinking all day, which I found to be an advantage. He was even more obnoxious than his usual self. I let him know that he had a choice to either leave with me or go directly to the hospital and then to jail. At that point, he pushed the owner aside, picked up a bottle, and started toward me from about twenty feet away. He was swaying from side to side and cursing, letting me know how he was going to put the bottle over my head. What he didn't realize was that I had nineteen undefeated amateur fights in a Golden Glove-type tournament in my younger days. I was also the heavyweight boxing champion of my police academy class. This was about to become very clear to him. He also didn't know that I was wearing sap gloves, which are leather gloves lined with small lead pellets.

Roy took two more steps toward me and began swinging the bottle. I immediately took a fighting stance, turning slightly to the right and taking one step back. He took his first swing with the bottle and missed. My right hand didn't. It caught him squarely in the nose. There was a crunching sound, which I knew meant that his nose was now broken. Clots of blood started to bubble out of his nostrils. His legs began to buckle and he staggered back two steps, but still refused to go down. He was wide-eyed, and his eyes glazed over. My left hand came up from my waist, catching him directly under his jaw. The chipped tooth he used to have existed no more and the size 16 construction boots flew off his feet. It was lights out for him. With his eyes fully rolled back in his head, he hit the floor on his back with a thundering thud.

I remember looking down at Roy and noticing that his socks had holes in them and his feet were flailing from side to side. As I rolled him over and cuffed him, he started to awaken and continued to scream obscenities at me. His wrists were so large, I couldn't get the cuffs to fit, so I stepped on them until I heard a click. He was transported under arrest to headquarters, where the first aid squad was standing by to take him to the hospital and attend to his medical needs. A few hours later, he was requesting to meet the officer who arrested him. I went to the cell area when my shift was ending and told him I was the one who put him in there. I fully expected some swearing and spitting and him telling me how he was going to kick my ass the next time we met. However, I found a very different person. His first words were, "I would like to apologize for my behavior. I was drunk and just showing off. Could you tell me your name?" I asked why and he admitted that it was the first time anyone had ever gotten the best of him. He told me that he would remember to be nicer to me the next time we crossed paths. Because of this incident, I now had a new nickname. They would call me "Lights Out."

Over the next few years, I would see Roy now and then and he was always respectful. If he was with anyone, he would say, "You see this man? This is the toughest guy I know, and if any of you ever disrespect him, you'll answer to me."

Fast forward about thirty years. My oldest son is a patrolman in the same town where I used to work. He stands about 5'10" and weighs around 240 pounds, with a crew-cut hairstyle. Some people call him a chip off the old block, only smaller. One day, he responded to a first aid call for a man having trouble breathing. It just so happened that the house he responded to was Leroy Blevens' and the man having the chest pains was Roy's younger brother. Upon arrival at the residence, my son received messages from other sector cars stating that they were en route to back him up. The patrolmen on their way were well aware of Roy's attitude toward police, so they were responding Code Red. My son had no idea what he was about to face and didn't know about the history between Roy and me.

He knocked on the door and heard the thunder of footsteps of someone approaching the door. As it opened, towering before him was a Goliath of a man, taking up the entire doorway. It was Leroy Blevens, who by then was about 340 pounds. Standing in his underwear, he looked at my son and said, "What do you want?" My son stated that he was there for a first aid call. Roy glared at him and then, seeing his nameplate, recognized the name Russell. His attitude quickly changed and he became much less hostile and more polite. He starting questioning my son and asked if he was related to me. When told that I was his father, he broke into a big smile and said, "I knew your father well. He was a hell of a guy. Please give him my regards and tell him Leroy was asking for him." My son was a little bewildered by this before asking where the person was with the breathing problem. Roy pointed to the back bedroom and let my son do his job.

As my son was administering oxygen to Roy's brother, he could hear multiple sirens, which he assumed was the first aid squad. Little did he know that it was three patrol cars, with two sergeants and a patrolman, along with an ambulance. The three police officers rushed into the residence, nightsticks in their hands, expecting a problem because of Roy's reputation of fighting with other police. Instead, they found a calm, beer-drinking mountain of a man watching television in his underwear and sitting in a recliner, pointing to the back bedroom. As they all left the house, Roy turned to my son and said, "Tell your dad I said hello." Standing outside by their cars, my son asked one of the sergeants the reason for so much backup. They then relayed the story about the time I knocked out Leroy Blevens. From that time on, my son thought I was a real badass.

CHAPTER 12
NIGHT COURT

"Your Honor, may we please approach the bench?" Sounds innocent enough, right? Far from it. The 12:00 am to 8:00 am shift is notoriously quiet after 3:00 am, but on occasion, it can be very busy. This was not one of those quiets nights. We were receiving calls about a male subject standing in the middle of the street and showing every indication that he was intoxicated. Headquarters dispatched two units, Danny Conway and Paul Kola, both big guys being well over six feet tall and weighing more than two hundred and fifty pounds each. They were fair but no-nonsense type of men. Upon arriving, sure enough, there was a man standing in the street and yelling at someone in the house located at 687 Perry Street. The officers determined that the man had had too much to drink and was staying at that address. Officer Conway convinced him to go back to the house and sleep it off, because if they had to come back, he would be arrested for disturbing the peace. The man complied and the units went back on patrol. One hour later, he was at it again, this time even more inebriated. I was at headquarters, the lieutenant had gone home early, and Sergeant Alfano was in charge of the station. He looked at me and commented, "How many times have we been at that house?" I told him it was twice that I knew of. He advised me to send Conway and Kola to bring the guy in, where he could sleep it off in the cell. Soon, the officers returned to headquarters with the screamer. He was placed in the cell and told to behave, but he kept up the screaming until Alfano had had enough. What happened next is what legends are made of.

I was told to go into the courtroom, put on the judge's robes, and just play along. Officer Kola went to the cell area and told the screaming guy that night court was in session and the judge wished to speak with him, because he was disturbing the court session and Judge Roy Bean was very angry. The judge, Kola warned him, wasn't someone to mess with and the best thing he could do was to say he was sorry and throw himself on the mercy of the court. The man asked what he thought the judge's sentence would be. Kola told him that he would most likely be told to be quiet and go back to the cell to sleep it off, and then he would probably be released in the morning.

The man was led into court a few minutes later. I was sitting at the bench, pretending to be the judge and looking very angry. I addressed him and demanded, "Do you have anything to say for yourself?" He replied very seriously, "Yes, your holiness. I apologize for all the noise. I was just celebrating and it got out of hand. I would like to throw myself on the mercy of the court." At this point, he looked at Kola and smiled. Kola grinned back and then they both turned toward the bench. The judge, which of course was me, stood and pointed at the man, telling him, "I believe you are sorry, but I feel I must make an example of you." The color drained from his face, turning it ashen. The judge further stated, "It is the decision of this court that the defendant be taken out back and hung for his crimes. This to be carried out at 7:00 am tomorrow morning." The man fell to his knees and began to really scream. Kola picked him up by his arms and said, with a nod towards me, "Sometimes he can be a real shit," and took him back to the cell.

At 6:00 am, Conway and Kola slipped into the cell area and opened the cell door, looking at the man who was now cold sober. "Listen," they told him, "the back door is open and we called a cab. Get in, go home, pack your stuff, and never come back to town again." The man gaped at them and replied, "You guys are real saints. Don't worry, you'll never see me again." With that, he hugged the two officers with appreciative tears in his eyes, quickly exited the cell, and made a beeline out of the building. He got into the waiting cab and, from what we understand, headed down to Florida where he had family and friends. Every time he heard a police siren or saw red lights in his mirror, I'm sure he worried whether it was him they were really after. I can't help but wonder if he ever got drunk and caused a public disturbance again. I don't think so.

CHAPTER 13
DOMESTIC DISTURBANCES

Domestic violence or abuse is "any abusive, violent, coercive, forceful, or threatening act or word inflicted by one member of a family or household on another." While at the academy, trainees attend classes on the handling of domestic violence calls. We are taught that this is one of the two most dangerous calls you can go on. One, because they can be threatening and two, because they are unpredictable. I was trained to always expect the unexpected because when responding to a domestic call, in a split second you can go from acting as a referee to becoming the victim.

One day, while working the day shift, I was driving through a shopping center and doing a routine patrol, looking for cars parked in a fire zone. The department had received an earlier call from the fire marshal, stating that there were numerous vehicles parked illegally in the fire zones and they wanted the vehicles ticketed, towed, or removed. As I drove, I noticed a man and woman having a heated, verbal argument between two parked cars.

I headed over to where the couple was and exited my car. The male was slight in build, approximately one hundred and thirty pounds. He was balding and appeared to be about forty years old. The female seemed to be around the same age and was wearing glasses, with her brown hair pulled back into a ponytail. She was much larger in size compared to the man, who immediately shouted to me, "Stay out of this. This is a private conversation between a husband and wife." I informed him that since his private conversation had become loud and started drawing the attention of a large group of shoppers, it was now becoming a public disturbance. The woman told me that she had a restraining order against him and that he was violating that order. He contended that there was no such order in place, but that she did owe him a large sum of money. I advised him if that was the case, he should seek the advice of an attorney and handle it through the court system, not in a parking lot.

At this point, the man became more agitated and started moving toward the woman. I warned him to back up and not to go any further. With his hand in his rear pants pocket, he appeared to be removing something – possibly keys or maybe even a weapon. It instantly became apparent that it was some sort of knife. As he raised his arm and lunged forward, I immediately stepped between them, trying to grab his arm. Attempting to strike the woman, he inadvertently slashed me from my right shoulder down to the left side of my waist with his silver box cutter, which was about six inches long with a razor attached to the tip. It was razor sharp and the only thing that saved me from being grievously injured was the fact that I was wearing my leather jacket over my vest, both of which took the full force of the slash. Quickly, my night stick came out, slamming into his wrist and breaking it. He fell to the ground, dropping the box cutter. While he screamed in pain, I grabbed him by the other wrist, turned him around, slammed him into his car door, cuffed him, and placed him under arrest. What had started out as a simple argument between two people turned into aggravated assault with a weapon on a police officer. The man was now facing lengthy prison time.

I was often reminded that any calls, first aid or other, to a residence could turn into a domestic violence incident. Because these circumstances can be so unpredictable, they may easily escalate into extremely volatile and dangerous situations. There was another occasion when I responded to a possible first aid call. Upon my arrival at the apartment in the Harbor Bay complex, I was approached by a female neighbor who claimed she had overheard someone yelling for help. The door was slightly ajar and I immediately knocked and identified myself as a police officer, asking if anyone needed help. I could hear what sounded like two people thrashing on the ground and a gurgling sound. I entered the residence and turned to my right, where I discovered two people on the floor. One was a burly, shirtless man who was sweating profusely. He was kneeling and straddling a female lying on her back. Her facial complexion was blue and I realized the man was tightly pulling on a telephone cord wrapped around her neck. I attempted to pull him off her, but he wouldn't release the phone cord. I pulled out my night stick and struck him, rendering him unconscious and causing him to roll off to the left.

I removed the cord from the woman's neck

and found she wasn't breathing. Within a minute or so of beginning mouth-to-mouth and CPR, the color started to return to her face and she was breathing on her own. The man was starting to regain consciousness, also, and attempted to kick me while I was trying to handcuff him. I placed my knee in the small of his back and advised him that he was under arrest. Just then, I felt a blow to my head. I became dazed and confused and could feel blood running down my face. I knew something was very wrong as I felt someone trying to pull my gun from my holster. Drifting out of consciousness, I kept a death grip on my gun as I began to pass out.

Apparently, a neighbor had heard the commotion and called the police department, alerting them that there was an officer in trouble and needed help. The next thing I recalled as I woke up was Officer Jake Lane kneeling beside me and applying a compress to my bleeding head. Becoming more alert, I asked him what had happened. He stated that he had arrived at the scene just in time. Evidently, he found the woman had struck me with a large and heavy glass ashtray and was attempting to grab my gun. He took two steps, pulled his night stick, and struck her across the head, dropping her to the floor. He then cuffed her and placed her under arrest before tending to my medical needs. He saved my life that night because had she gotten my gun, I have no doubt that she would have shot and killed me.

When I went to court the next day for an arraignment hearing, I testified before Judge McCarthy to the actions of both the man and woman. Officer Lane testified, as well. The judge was dumbfounded as he read the facts of the case and stated that in all the years he had served on the bench, this was without a doubt the most difficult to comprehend. He pointed to the woman and said, "One of my officers here literally saved your life by not only stopping someone from strangling you with a telephone cord, but then by giving you mouth-to-mouth resuscitation to revive you. You then assault him and try to take his weapon – to do what? Shoot him? I find your actions to be most disturbing." Addressing them both, he continued, "It is the verdict of this court to have you both remanded to the county jail, where you, sir, will be charged for attempted murder on this woman and you, madam, will be charged with aggravated assault, causing bodily harm with the use of a weapon on a police officer."

Several days later, while recalling the

incidents that took place, I reflected on what I could have done differently. Everything I had done during that call was textbook, right up to the point where I was struck in the head by the victim. There is no way I could have ever imagined that the victim would become the aggressor toward me. After all, I had just saved her life. This is exactly what I meant earlier about domestic violence. These calls can be so unpredictable and dangerous that one second you are breaking up an argument, and the next second you have become a victim.

CHAPTER 14
THE BIRTH OF "THE LEGEND"

Every city and town has their own group of gangs, and we were no exception. Usually, a town will only have one major gang because they don't allow other gangs to invade their home turf. What made our town different was the fact that we had two motorcycle gangs. This stemmed from years earlier, when we had one large gang called the Road Kings, comprised of more than four hundred members. There was an internal conflict regarding who would control the hierarchy of the gang and this internal fighting eventually turned into a full-scale war. As the story was relayed to me, the group was having their annual picnic bash at McGovern's Grove, which was a local park where you could rent out sections for your function. Apparently, after hours of drinking, a heated and physical altercation took place, leading to the state police and five neighboring departments to respond. Numerous arrests were made for assaults, aggravated assaults, and weapons charges. It was reported that two deaths and multiple gunshot wounds took place at this incident. This was the beginning of the splinter group known as the War Lords.

The War Lords were a "wannabe" group of the Road Kings. They made a lot of noise and threatened some of the local residents with their own tales and exploits of how bad they were. This ultimately enraged the Road Kings, who were a much larger group almost twice their size. All law enforcement kept their eyes on both groups due to their use of guns and drug trafficking. Several members were also arrested for killing a truck driver who had dis-respected one of the female members.

One particular night at Billy Ray's Bar was the monthly meeting of the War Lords, the smaller splinter group that had branched out on their own. They had been given notice by the Road Kings to discontinue any meetings whatsoever in town, but this went unheeded. They would not allow locals or anyone else to be in the bar while the meeting was taking place because it was a private function for members only. The topics of discussion included drugs, the sale of weapons, and human trafficking.

That night, it seemed that some of the local barflies were having a little party of their own and didn't want to leave just yet, even as the War Lords were arriving. The gang didn't want the twenty-five or so locals present to witness their business agenda. When the War Lords ordered everyone to "Get the fuck out," all hell broke loose. It began as a pushing and shoving match between the customers and some of the members. This then escalated into objects being thrown, including billiard balls, bottles, glasses, bar stools, and chairs, plus some people being thrown in the air. Somehow, someone from within the bar was able to get to the phone in the back office (remember, cell phones hadn't been invented yet) and call the police to tell them that a massive fight had broken out. Help was needed specifically because the War Lords were involved.

When I received the dispatch call, I was only moments away. As I approached the bar in my vehicle, I heard a loud and thunderous crash of glass. Looking up, I saw that a bar stool had just been thrown through the front window. I immediately called for assistance without knowing what the situation was, but I could hear and see the commotion as well as the many motorcycles in the parking lot. I entered through the open side door, where some customers were now fleeing the melee inside. Once in, all I could see was a massive amount of fighting making its way toward me.

I announced that I was with the police department, which only infuriated the crowd more and escalated the situation. I had my nightstick in my right hand and grabbed a chair with my left, backing myself into a corner where no one could get behind me and allowing a panoramic view of what was going on in front of me. A billiard ball flew by my head, embedding itself into the sheetrock behind me. Two War Lords were approaching me, one carrying a pool stick and the other a broken beer bottle. With my nightstick, I struck the one with the pool stick on the wrist and heard it break. He immediately screamed in pain and collapsed to the floor. The other guy lunged forward with his broken bottle, missing me and hitting the chair that I was holding for protection. I swung my nightstick again, striking him in the collarbone once and causing him to drop what was left of his bottle. I then struck him again on the side of his face between the ear and eye. He collapsed straight to the floor.

There was still a full-scale brawl taking place around me. Moving to the right and stepping over bodies on the floor, I received a blow to my chest by someone coming from my blind side, which staggered me for a moment. My biggest fear throughout all this was that someone would try to grab my gun from my holster, then use it as a weapon on me. I could feel hands pulling at my uniform shirt. My first response was to keep swinging my nightstick at anything within my reach.

The sounds of the brawl were beginning to lessen, maybe because there were more bodies on the floor than standing up. I heard sirens in the distance and knew help was coming fast. I could also hear the moaning and groaning of injured people and there was blood everywhere. I took a quick inventory of myself, finding that my shirt had been ripped off my body, my badge was missing, and I was covered in blood. Thank God, none of it was mine. My eyes met those of the bartender, who had poked up his head after hiding behind the bar. He had a look of terror and surprise on his face, wondering how I had survived and was still standing. Just then, entering through the front door and stepping over bodies, Jake Lane, Joe Polk, Danny Conway, and Sergeant Alfano arrived. They looked at me, surveyed the room, and asked if I was all right. After I assured them I was fine, Jake smiled and pointed around, asking, "Did you fucking do this?" The bartender yelled out, "I saw everything. He was great. I've never seen anything like it in my life." In reality, he saw nothing and I was only responsible for dropping about four guys during the fight. Nevertheless, "The Legend" was born. Before leaving the bar, I scanned the floor and found what was left of my shirt, with my badge attached to it. After going outside and being attended to and cleared by the first aid squad, I returned to headquarters, put on a new shirt, pinned my badge back on, and resumed my patrol.

As time went on, the story of that infamous brawl got bigger and better. I once heard it told that I beat up thirty War Lords and shot three. I would just smile and say, "Things happen in the midst of a fight and for the life of me, I can't remember all the details of that night." From that night on, I actually earned three new nicknames. One was Mad Dog, the second was Lights Out, and the third, of course, was The Legend.

A few weeks later on the other side of town, the Road Kings were having a fundraiser at Rooney's Monkey Bar. This was a topless bar known for its dancers, who were very well endowed. When you have an event with alcohol, nudity, and the Road Kings, you have the ingredients that make up a "trifecta," which guarantees a disturbance call. Sure enough, the call came in at 1:00 am, dispatching a sector car for a noise violation. This time, Jake Lane was the first to respond. He had a natural dislike for the Road Kings due to an incident that had happened several years earlier. Because he had been on several calls earlier that night, his patience was running low. Sergeant Alfano knew this, so he also dispatched me, knowing I would be just a few minutes behind Jake. When I entered the bar, I noticed that Jake was in a heated conversation with the president of the Road Kings, Willie St. Clair. This guy stood about six feet seven inches and weighed well over three hundred pounds, with long black hair pulled back in a ponytail. He was wearing an American flag bandana, which was his signature piece of clothing. His arms were huge and could be described as tree trunks, and were covered with tattoos. He had the demeanor of a rabid pit bull and had earned his position as head of the Road Kings by physically kicking anyone's ass who tried to challenge his authority.

Jake had been advising Willie that, because of several complaints, they would either have to settle down or the party would be broken up and declared over. The conversation was becoming confrontational and Jake's night-stick was already out and in his hand. I did not want a repeat of the War Lords brawl that had occurred a few weeks earlier. Just then, Willie took a step closer to Jake. His eyes were no longer looking at Jake, but were now fixed on me. As I headed toward the two of them, hoping to diffuse the situation, Willie looked at me and said, "Officer Russell, I didn't see you come in. Welcome to our little party. What can I do for you?" I told him that I was just there to make sure there were no problems. Willie stepped around Jake and commented that they had heard about the War Lords incident and that if I ever had a problem with that gang in the future, to please give him a call. I thanked him for the offer, but respectfully declined.

The crowd around us had been anticipating a physical altercation and the bar had become completely silent, with no music and no dancing girls – just a bunch of eyes on Willie, Jake, and me. Willie extended his hand to shake mine and assured me that they would settle down and there would be no further problems.

As Jake and I left, I turned to him and smiled, "Once again, the Legend lives on." We laughed as we climbed into our cars and resumed patrol without further incidents that night.

CHAPTER 15
MY GUARDIAN ANGEL

Throughout my life, I have always believed that there was a guardian angel looking over me. When I graduated from the police academy, my parents gave me a gold chain with a pendent of St. Michael the Archangel, which I immediately wore around my neck and never took off. He is the patron saint of police officers who is said to give us strength, courage, and protection during critical or dangerous times. There have been numerous situations when I felt his presence watching over and guiding me. This was one of those times.

One night, I was getting ready to begin my tour. It was about 10:00 pm and I worked the midnight shift. I was about to leave home and I recall having a feeling that I had forgotten something. I checked my duty bag and everything appeared to be there, so I dismissed the feeling and continued on my way. Arriving at work, the strange feeling persisted but I couldn't put my finger on it. I was sitting next to Joe Morris in the muster room, which is a squad room where your shift assignments are given. Joe asked, "You alright? Is something bothering you?" I nodded and told him that I couldn't explain it, but I would be fine.

That nagging, hair-raised-on-the-back-of-the-neck feeling lasted a couple more hours before I realized that my Gerber pocketknife was missing. I kept this knife in a watch pocket just below my duty belt line. It was given to me by my father, who had carried it himself while serving in World War II. He had told me, "Always carry this, because you never know when you might need it. It saved my ass many years ago and it could save yours." When I realized the knife was not where it should be, I immediately pulled my car over to the side of the road and opened the duty bag, searching through all the pockets until I found it. Somehow, it had wedged itself into a small pocket and I had missed it on the first check. Putting it back in my watch pocket where it belonged, I went on my way and that nagging uneasiness subsided.

At about 3:30 am, I received a call that there was an accident on Route 37 that involved multiple vehicles and minor injuries. Responding code three, which means red lights and sirens, I arrived at the scene and began to assess the situation. I called for the tow trucks and for the first aid squad to attend to the injured parties. Thankfully, the injuries were not serious; just some minor cuts and bruises, and only one vehicle needed to be towed. Once the accident was cleared, I pulled the patrol car onto the shoulder of the road so I could finish the accident report.

All of a sudden, I could see in the distance headlights approaching from my rear view mirror. I was still buckled in with my seat belt on. A small delivery box truck, similar to a U-Haul vehicle, that was carrying produce veered onto the shoulder and slammed into the rear of my patrol car, sending my vehicle tumbling over and landing on its roof. The driver had fallen asleep behind the wheel and drifted onto the shoulder. I recall feeling disoriented because I was hanging upside down with my seat belt still attached. I was happy to be alive and I knew the seat belt had saved my life. Had I not been wearing it, the impact probably would have thrown me through the windshield and most likely would have killed me. I tried to release the seat belt so I could escape, but it was mangled and jammed and I couldn't release it. I could smell the fumes of the gasoline that was flooding into my car. The violent crash had ruptured the fuel tank and I was still trapped. I was feeling light-headed and dizzy and noticed that the battery cables were beginning to spark. I knew if those sparks hit the gasoline, the car would explode like fireworks on the Fourth of July. While still struggling to free myself, I noticed that my St. Michael medal was hanging in my face. I immediately heard a little voice in my head, which I believe was my guardian angel, and he was telling me to use the Gerber knife. Reaching into my watch pocket, I pulled out my knife, which was small but razor sharp. It cut through the seat belt like a hot knife through butter. As the belt released me from my seat, I tried to push open the door, but it was jammed. The only other way out was to roll through the opening of the shattered driver's side window. I crawled on my hands and knees and dragged myself through broken glass and debris, getting as much distance as possible between me and the car that I knew would explode at any moment. Within seconds, there was a tremendous boom and as I looked back, I saw my car engulfed in flames. Staring at the burning vehicle, I felt a calming presence. Reaching under my shirt, I clutched my St. Michael pendant and thanked him for watching over and protecting me. I realized that my father was right. That Gerber knife did save my ass.

Many years later, while my wife and I were traveling from Tampa to New Jersey, I forgot that I had the knife in the pocket of the cargo pants I was wearing. As we went through security at the airport, the alarm sounded and I was taken out of line and asked if I had anything in my pockets. I replied, "No." The TSA agent used his metal detector wand to see if he could find the source. Sure enough, deep down in one of the pockets, there was the Gerber knife. The TSA agent informed me he would have to confiscate it. I showed him my retired badge and told him there was no way I was giving up that knife. The agent happened to be a retired New York City policeman and when I told him the story behind the knife, he replied, "If it was my knife, I wouldn't give it up, either." I asked how we could remedy the problem and the solution was clear. He handed me a small manila envelope to place the knife inside and asked me to address it to where I wanted it sent. I wrote my son's address, which was where we were staying in New Jersey, and I paid the postage right there. The agent mailed it and three days later, I was re-united with it. That was the only time that I have ever been separated from my knife. To this day, I still wear that pendant and carry that knife with me. Like Dad said, "You never know when you'll need it again."

CHAPTER 16
THE SHOOT-OUT

During those days at the police academy, when every instructor is flooding your brain with information on how to make you a better and safer officer, you sometimes wonder, "Is all of this necessary?" I can tell you now: Yes, it is. The day will come when that small piece of information that you thought was a waste of time could actually save your life. As a police officer, you are trained to always expect the unexpected and your instincts become second nature. You'll find yourself doing things that, later on, you won't remember planning to do; you'll just automatically do them. We received the best training that was available by the best instructors.

I had been on the job for about two years and one night, I had just finished making my rounds of the stores in my sector. Midnight tour made you feel like a night watchman because you were always checking doors, windows, schools, and basically anything else that was locked. There were some stores that were open 24/7 every day. I looked forward to checking in with them so I could talk to somebody, which made the night go faster. On this particular night, I had just stopped at the 7-11 store on County Highway 472. The night clerk, named Harry Brennan, was a retired fireman who worked part time so he could have some extra spending money. Harry was about 5'10" with a slight build, weighing about 160 pounds. He had a crewcut with salt and pepper hair and always wore this big smile, which instantly drew you into wanting to have a conversation with him. He always greeted anyone and everyone who walked into the store, "Hey, how ya doing today?" Police officers were always known as "the finest" and firemen were known as "the bravest," so Harry and I would often joke or poke fun at each other as to who was better. We would talk about his time in Engine Company 24, which was one of the busiest engine companies in the town. His stories were usually the best, since I wasn't on the force that long.

After picking up my coffee that night, I

asked Harry if he would be working the next day and after he confirmed that he was, I said I would see him then. Little did I know I would see him a lot sooner and under a much different set of circumstances.

It was 3:00 am and Harry's parking lot was empty, but as I left the store, I noticed a car parked on the shoulder of the road with its lights out, about fifty yards away. I didn't recall it being there when I went in to see Harry, so I drove to the first intersection and made a left. Turning out my lights, I circled back and parked in a lot at a doctor's office across from the 7-11, where I could observe the store and the car at the same time. I could see the vehicle but he could not see me. It wasn't long before the driver put on his lights and drove very slowly, pulling into the store parking lot. He went all the way to the far corner of the lot and just sat there, which was unusual because at that time of night, most cars would park right in front of the door. His lights went off, but the car was still running and I could see the exhaust pipes smoking. Instincts took over and I knew something was wrong.

I called Sergeant Alfano, briefed him on the situation, and told him that I thought that a 10-38, which is a holdup and robbery, was about to happen. He instructed other units to respond quietly and started to direct cars into that area – one on each side of the store, two in the rear, and one more with me across the street. The driver finally opened his door and stood outside, peering in the store windows. He wore a navy knit cap, black denim jeans, and a black jacket. All of a sudden, he tugged the cap down over his face and pulled a sawed-off shotgun from under his jacket. I immediately radioed in that the robbery was going down and was now in progress.

The man strode into the store and I could see that Harry had thrown his hands up in the air, with the shotgun pointed directly at him. I wanted to rush inside, but was advised by Alfano to stand by until the suspect came out because we didn't want this becoming a hostage situation. It was difficult for me to wait because I feared for Harry's life. I didn't want him being shot and I knew if that happened, I would never be able to live with the guilt if I just held back and watched him be killed. After Harry gave him a brown bag, the man slowly backed up toward the front door, still pointing the gun, then turned quickly to exit.

Through the window, I could see Harry heading toward the rear of the store. Putting our cars in gear, Officer Ted Roland and I rapidly crossed the highway and positioned our cars facing the front entrance. When the suspect emerged, he came face to face with two police officers behind their patrol cars with their guns drawn, plus more police on each side of the building. I shouted, "Put down the weapon and the bag and put your hands up in the air!" He just stood there looking at us, with his gun still in hand. I ordered a second time, "Put the weapon down! There is nowhere to go." Then he did something incredibly stupid. Instead of putting the shotgun down, he raised it waist high and a single blast went off, with pellets striking the ground in front of the police cars. That prompted all of us to return fire, striking him four times. The scene suddenly became very quiet as the suspect dropped the gun and bag, removed his cap, and sat on the sidewalk. He muttered, "I can't believe you shot me. I wasn't supposed to get shot," before he fell backward and just lay there. We approached him, cuffed him, removed the weapon by his side, and called for first aid.

When all was said and done, Harry was safe, the incident was over, no police officers were injured, and the suspect, who was shot four times and eventually recovered, served thirty years in the state prison for armed holdup and robbery and attempted murder of a police officer. I don't think this man realized that the rest of his life would be forever changed after robbing a store for just $57, the exact tally of money that was in the bag. After that night, when Harry and I would jokingly talk about who was the finest or bravest, he would agree I was "the finest." Ironically, in all of my thirty-seven years of serving on the job, that would be the only time I ever had to fire my weapon. I thank God for that.

CHAPTER 17
HEATHER JENNINGS

Over the course of your career as a police officer, you will run the full gamut of emotions. Some will bring great satisfaction for a job well done and others will keep you laughing with a lingering smile on your face. There will be promotions as well as some complaints. Hopefully, the complaints will be kept to a minimum. There will also be some terrible tragedies that you will never be able to erase from your mind. What I'm about to relate to you is one of those tragedies that, to this day, still haunts me.

It was in the summer of my third year on the job, and I hoped that the terrible sights I had experienced were beginning to taper off. My hope was short-lived. While working the day shift, I had just finished up in court, which was in the same complex as headquarters, and was leaving to resume my patrol. As I entered my patrol car, I heard dispatch call the sector car in reference to a first aid call; a baby was choking. The address was in the apartment building right behind headquarters. The sector car was a few minutes away and since time was critical, I responded, "Headquarters, 517 is closer." Dispatch confirmed, "10-4, you respond." When I arrived at the apartment, I found a young woman in her early twenties. She was wearing a bathrobe and crying hysterically as she pressed her infant closely to her chest. I asked her to give me the baby, but she was reluctant. I insisted because her infant, who was about three months old, appeared to be blue and not breathing. I ran into the kitchen, placing the baby girl onto the table. I checked the child's mouth to see if she was choking on anything, but could see no obstructions. I began to perform CPR and, after a few moments, the baby took a breath on her own and opened her eyes slightly, so I immediately stopped. I thought everything was going to be fine, but then she stopped breathing again. I resumed giving her CPR and the child started to vomit up formula and mucous while making gurgling sounds. The first aid squad arrived and we rushed the baby to the ambulance. I gave them a police escort all the way to the hospital, where the doctors took over and I stayed in the waiting room with the mother. I asked her about the incident and she told me that she had just finished feeding the baby, so she laid the child on the couch next to her while she read the newspaper. She remembered looking at the clock and it was 10:30 am. The next thing she remembered was that it was 11:15 am and the baby was face down on the floor next to the couch and not breathing. She didn't know how the baby got there. That's when she called for help.

One of the doctors came into the waiting room and asked who the mother was. I pointed to the woman seated next to me. The doctor sat down, took the woman's hand, and said, "I'm truly sorry. Your child expired a few minutes ago." I consoled the mother in my arms for a few minutes before one of the nurses came over and asked if she could call someone for her. Then the doctor motioned that he wanted to speak to me outside. As we walked away, he stated, "That child has severe head and neck trauma. There is also bruising around the baby's ankles." He thought there was abuse involved and that detectives should be called in to investigate. A detective soon arrived at the hospital and took the woman to headquarters for questioning. I couldn't get that unaccounted forty-five minutes out of my head and wondered, "Why did it take her so long to call?" I mentioned this to the detective before he left the hospital. The mother was later released to a family member and told to be available for more possible questions.

The next day, Detective DePasquale called me into his office and told me, "I could see in your eyes that the baby call from yesterday was getting to you. I just wanted to let you know there was nothing more you could have done." DePasquale had gone to the autopsy earlier that morning because it was a suspicious death of a child and a possible homicide. The autopsy revealed that the child actually died of extreme head trauma, including neck and spine injuries, and wanted me to know this. Upon the results of the medical findings, the mother was brought back to headquarters for further interrogation. During that questioning, DePasquale attempted to fill in the blanks as to what happened during that forty-five minute blackout or time gap. He asked her about her medical history and she informed him that when she was seventeen years old, she experimented with LSD – otherwise known as acid, which is a mind-altering drug. This had caused a hallucinogenic experience or "trip," which resulted in her emotional inability to recognize reality or think rationally. She had to be hospitalized as a result. This scared her so profoundly that she never used it again. However, the sad part in all of this is that taking LSD can cause extreme long-term effects. Some of them include sudden flashbacks without warning or blackouts, and may also manifest relatively long-lasting psychoses, such as schizophrenia or severe depression. Through further questioning by Detective DePasquale, the woman slowly began to recall that gap in time. She thought she saw snakes coming out of the couch to attack the baby, so she picked up the rolled newspaper to swat them away. In reality, she had grabbed the baby by the ankles and attempted to kill the snakes. Apparently, she had had a flashback that was a recurrence of the effects of the LSD that she had taken years earlier.

After having all the facts and speaking with the prosecutor, the mother was charged with involuntary manslaughter and held for psychological evaluation. I cannot impress upon the young people of today that their actions can sometimes have terrible consequences for which they will be held accountable. In this case, a young woman who did something stupid years earlier now has to live for the rest of her life with the guilt of accidentally killing her own daughter and has destroyed her own life. I am forever haunted by the face of that beautiful little baby. Her name was Heather Jennings.

CHAPTER 18
MY FIRST PROMOTION

It was hard to believe that almost five years had gone by on the job. I felt like I gained a wealth of knowledge through the many personal interactions I had with the public as a police officer. This included traffic stops, domestic disturbance calls, drug trafficking, bank robberies, house fires, and even delivering a baby. After being sheltered from seeing some things as a civilian, I was seeing the world with new eyes, but there was always a part of me that strived to be better and I remembered my father's words to me on my graduation day from the academy. He always said, "Reach for the stars."

The previous month, I had seen a posting that a sergeants test was going to be given. I thought it might be a good idea to take it, but I had my concerns due to only having five years on the job. There were many officers with much more seniority that would be taking the test, so I thought my chances would be slim. However, I was encouraged by Deputy Chief Baldwin to take the exam. He thought there was something special about me and that I would make a good supervisor since I was objective and had a good working relationship with the public and my fellow colleagues. The deputy chief had basically mentored me since I came on the job and because I valued his opinion, I decided to move forward with the test.

There were three phases of the test. The first was a written test of one hundred questions. To prepare myself for this part, I enrolled in a study program that was strictly geared toward police testing. My preparation and routine included driving to the school and spending three hours a day there, three days a week, for three weeks. Part of the program was having a high-ranking instructor, usually a lieutenant or captain not from my department, who would review questions that could possibly be on the test. These were general knowledge questions, with a few situational questions thrown in. The testing would take about three hours and would be difficult, so

I wanted to be disciplined in studying for the first phase. If I didn't pass the test with a high enough score, I would not be able to move on.

The second phase of the test was an oral exam. For that, you would meet before a review board consisting of two captains and a lieutenant from other police departments. They would ask situational questions such as, "How would you handle a hostage situation? How would you set up a perimeter during a bank robbery? How would you handle a major disaster?" They also wanted to know how you would handle evaluations of officers under your direct control. Your answers gave the review board insight as to how good you might be during high-stress situations.

Phase three was a psychological evaluation given by an accredited psychologist. He would determine how you might process certain situations that required high mental stress. One possible scenario included how you would handle the fatal shooting of a fellow officer. Another was what your mental state would be if you were skipped over for a promotion. There were also general questions about your marriage, your family, whether you had children, relationships you had in general, and what other activities you participated in outside of the police department. I remember him asking me about my son, who was going through childhood cancer. This doctor really delved into how your life outside the police department might affect your decision-making process as a supervisor.

When the scores were posted, I was shocked and surprised that I had done so well. I came in second highest with a cumulative score of 94.5, just missing the number one score by one point. About twenty-five senior patrolmen had taken the test, so I was ecstatic. Everyone's results were posted in order, from highest to lowest. The entire department knew that three sergeants were going to be made and with me being second on the list, it was a sure thing. The same night that the posting was made, a group of fellow officers took me out to a local bar to celebrate my soon-to-be new stripes. My sergeant even came to the bar and presented me a pair of his gold collar sergeant stripes because he thought I would be promoted within the week and he wanted to be first to congratulate me.

That following Monday, the sergeants would be officially promoted at a council meeting by the chief of police. On the previous night, I received a phone call from Deputy Chief

Baldwin. He asked if we could meet for coffee at the local diner. Obviously, I agreed because I thought he wanted to congratulate me and review the proceedings of the promotional process that would be taking place the next day. When I arrived at the diner, I was surprised by his demeanor. He looked depressed and serious, which gave me cause for concern. He motioned for me to sit down and said that he wanted me to listen and to remember that this was not the end of the road, but the beginning. I was confused and upset because I didn't know where this was going. I had my suspicions, but dismissed them because it couldn't possibly be so. He looked directly into my eyes and said, "Your promotion is not happening tomorrow night." As my heart sank into my stomach, my first question was, "How could this possibly be?" He replied, "You're going to find, especially in this business, that politics become involved and unfortunately for you, we have had to make some changes. There is a silver lining in this. I want you to do me a personal favor and have some patience and say nothing about what I am about to tell you." He then informed me that Sergeant Dempsey had put in his papers on Friday and would be leaving the first of the next month. That meant another position would open up and at that time, I would be promoted and get my sergeant stripes. As devastated as I was because I knew I deserved the promotion, I understood that because of politics, certain concessions had to be made. I wanted to come across as a team player and I respected Baldwin immensely, so I went along with the plan for me to step aside this once.

When I eventually got promoted a month later, my hurt and disappointment subsided because I was officially a sergeant and supervisor. Before new sergeants received their squad assignments, it was mandatory to appear before the chief. Being a little nervous going to see him and not knowing what to expect, it was a little unsettling. As I sat waiting to meet with him, I heard a voice over the intercom asking if Sergeant Russell was out there. His secretary confirmed and with that, I was called into his office. As I entered, I saw the chief sitting at his massive desk. Glancing over the top of his glasses, he gave me a visual inspection, looking me up one side and down the other. He gave a half-assed smirk and I knew he approved. He was not a physically intimidating figure – about 5'9" and very slim – but one look from him could stop you dead in your tracks. He was bald and constantly had a small stub of a cigar stuck out of the corner of his mouth.

Without removing his cigar, the chief began to speak. His gravelly voice always made
him sound angry. He was truly old school and
started to lay down the law, stating what he
expected and making it perfectly clear that he
had high expectations of me. I was told that
I was replacing Sergeant Dempsey, who was
one of the best, and that I had big shoes to fill.
After about twenty minutes or so, he rose and
extended his hand to shake mine, saying, "I
wish you all the best. Check in with Lieutenant
Quinn and remember, I'll be watching." I left
his office and breathed a sigh of relief. Then
slowly it hit me; I was no longer responsible
for just myself, but for eight additional officers.
I was now going to be judged on how well my
officers performed, both good and bad.

Heading to the watch commander's office,
I saw Lieutenant Quinn standing in the doorway. His voice rang out, "Sergeant Russell,
get in here." Because he was a massive giant
of a man, you automatically listened when he
spoke. He stood about 6'6" tall, weighing in at
about two hundred seventy-five pounds without one ounce of fat on him. He had a weathered complexion and what stood out most
about him were his hands. Everyone called
them "ham hands," but never to his face, and
when he shook yours, he almost crushed it

with his vice-like grip. In his office, he gave me my squad assignment, which was B Squad. This was made up of all senior officers, each having more than ten years of experience. I knew they might have some resentment about taking orders from a supervisor with only five years of experience, an amount that was at least half of theirs. I wasn't sure how I was going to handle this.

My first tour as a sergeant was the busy 4:00 pm to 12:00 midnight shift. I arrived early, at 3:00 pm, as most supervisors did. I wanted to speak with my old boss Sergeant Alfano, who was sitting at the sergeant's desk when I came in. Looking up, he said, "Well, look what we have here. New stripes, new badge, all shined up, and looking good. All kidding aside – congratulations. Just call me with whatever help you need." Checking over my roster, he shook his head and told me, "You're going to have some problems with this bunch. Some are already sounding off about having some-one with only five years of experience telling them what to do." His only advice was to let them know upfront that I was the boss and would run this squad fairly and intelligently; if they had any problems, we would air them out immediately before hitting the streets.

After Sergeant Alfano's squad passed along all their past tour information, I was left alone with my men. I gave them my speech about cooperation and working together and that respect was earned. I then asked if there were any questions, but there were none. They received their sector assignments and the shift started without so much as a peep. I was hoping this wouldn't be the calm before the storm. There might always be that look of resentment, but it was never verbalized and they did their jobs well.

Two months had passed without incident and then I received notice to report to Lieutenant Quinn's office before the start of my next tour. What was all this about? As I approached, he said, "Come in and sit down. I have something to ask you." He continued, "The chief wants to know if you would be willing to change squads." I asked if there been any complaints. He told me that, on the contrary, I had gotten great evaluations from shift commanders and the division commander. He explained, "As you know, we are putting six officers through the academy and they are graduating in two weeks. The chief thinks you would be a perfect fit to take all of them and mold them into one of our new squads. You would also be able to pick your number two – preferably, someone with training background and at least five years of experience. He would like your answer today. This way, I can get your transfer and their assignments ready to go." Naturally, I said yes. I knew my number two would be Officer Joe Morris and when I told Quinn, he smiled and agreed, "Good choice. That's who I would have picked." Two weeks came quickly and my new bunch of "fire breathers" was assigned. A lifelong brotherhood of the best squad our department had ever seen was about to begin.

CHAPTER 19
MY ITALIAN TRANSLATOR

When I reflect on the early days of preparing my new squad for the intense world of police work, I have to laugh at some of those memories. One such experience was night court. Part of my responsibilities as a sergeant was to train my officers on how to properly testify in court. It seemed that when the newer patrolmen testified in court, they would sometimes drift from the law and give their personal opinion or judgement. They would also ramble on without getting straight to the point. This would often lead to confusing testimony and, ultimately, the defense attorneys would damage the officers' credibility. For this reason, I thought it was important to take three or four of my officers into court every now and then to have them listen to the proper way in which a good officer should testify. Part of their learning process included knowing what to say and what not to say. Officers testifying were required to give a complete report or account on whatever their actions were on a particular occasion. This would be based on fact and not on speculation. If a judge should ask for your professional opinion, then it would be acceptable to elaborate and this would make it admissible in court.

I remember one particular night when I brought several of my officers into court strictly to observe. I always had them sit together alongside of me in case they had any particular questions. A simple assault case was currently on the docket. It seemed that two next-door neighbors got into an argument over where their property boundary lines began and ended. The prosecutor was asking the victim, Mr. Salpietro, to tell the court in his own words what had happened on the day of the incident. The man stated that he was mowing his lawn when his neighbor Mr. Camasta, who had been working on his car, came over and began yelling at him. Mr. Salpietro couldn't quite hear or understand what his neighbor was saying because of the noise level of the lawn mower. Mr. Camasta then started shaking his fist in a manner that made Mr. Salpietro think he would be hit. At that point, he stopped his mower and asked what the problem was. His neighbor's face turned beet red and he angrily headed with a crowbar toward Mr. Salpietro, who told him to get off his property or he would call the police. Mr. Camasta struck him on the shoulder with the crow bar. The prosecutor asked if there was anything else he wanted to add, but Mr. Salpietro replied, "No, sir. That is the way I remember it."

Then it was time for Mr. Camasta, the defendant, to take the stand and tell his side of the incident the way he remembered it. As he sat in the chair alongside the judge, the prosecutor asked him, "Mr. Camasta, please tell the court your side of the incident." There was a long silence. Mr. Camasta just sat there, silently staring at the judge with a bewildered look on his face.

Now, the court was extremely crowded on this night, with about one hundred people in the gallery. Everyone was looking at each other, wondering why the witness wasn't responding. Finally, the judge turned to the prosecutor and asked, "Does this man understand English? He seems confused." After a few moments, it was determined that Mr. Camasta didn't speak or understand English very well and apparently only spoke Italian. The judge looked around the room and asked if there was anyone present that could speak Italian. For a moment, no one answered. Then one of my officers, who was sitting in the front row, raised his hand and said, "Your Honor, I speak Italian." Because he was sitting furthest away from me, I couldn't question him about being an interpreter and I had no idea he could speak fluent Italian. The next thing I knew, the judge summoned my officer to come forward and to sit next to the witness. Peering over the top of his glasses, the judge asked, "What is your name, officer, for the record?" He replied, "My name is Officer Carelli." The judge instructed him to ask Mr. Camasta if he had struck Mr. Salpietro with a crowbar. Officer Carelli nodded, turned to the defendant, and asked, "Didda you a hitta himma witha the crowbar?" The room went deathly silent and I couldn't believe what I had just heard. It was the worst mangling of the Italian language I had ever heard. At that moment, the judge looked at me and shook his head.

You should know that Judge Sweeney was an absolutely no-nonsense judge. He treated his court in the most reverent manner and when anyone entered his courtroom, they had better give the respect which he felt it required. Judge Sweeney pushed back his chair, took off his glasses, rubbed his eyes, and said, "Sergeant Russell, would you please thank Officer Carelli for all of his expertise in helping to translate for the court? It was greatly appreciated." As the officer was stepping down from the stand and walking back to his seat, you could hear the sound of laughter starting from the crowd. This only infuriated the judge even more. Before Officer Carelli got to his seat, I told him to meet me outside the courtroom so we could have a talk. He clearly didn't have a clue as to what he had done wrong, why people were laughing, and why I wanted to speak with him. Once we got in the lobby, I grabbed him by the shirt and demanded, "What in God's name was that? Did you really believe that just by adding the letter "A" after every word, it meant you could speak Italian? Are you fucking kidding me?" He responded that his Italian grandfather spoke to him that way, so he assumed that all Italians spoke that way, as well. I was so embarrassed and angry that all I could tell him was to go back on patrol and we would continue the discussion later. My biggest fear then was that I knew I had to go back into the courtroom because I still had three officers sitting in the front row. God only knew what trouble they could get into without me being there after seeing what happened with Officer Carelli.

It seemed like the longest walk I ever made was that walk back down to my seat as I entered the courtroom. There was still some snickering, muttering, and laughter going on before the judge slammed down his gavel, silencing the crowd, and warned, "I'll have no more of that." Once seated, I looked at my officers who were smiling and told them, "Wipe that smile off your face now." Then I noticed that the judge motioned the bailiff to the bench and handed him a note, which was brought to me. It simply said, "I wish to see you in my chambers when court is over."

After court, I joined the judge in chambers. He was furious because he believed Officer Carelli had made a mockery of his courtroom and I was responsible for my men. I explained to the judge that I brought my men to court so they could properly learn how to testify and was shocked when Carelli volunteered to assist. I told the judge that I had spoken with the officer after the incident and he had assured me that he meant no disrespect, that he was merely trying to help, and that apparently his family, who were mostly Italian, spoke mixed Italian and English so he assumed this was the proper way. The judge advised me that a full report of this incident would be sent to the chief. He added that the next time I decided to take my men to court to observe, it had better be on a day when he was not on the bench. I apologized profusely and assured him that this would never happen again. He dismissed me and I humbly thanked him, turned, and left his chambers.

CHAPTER 20
ANSWER TO MY PRAYERS

It was 1975 and shortly after becoming a sergeant, my priorities started to change. I was in a struggling marriage, I had a son who was not quite two years old, and my wife was pregnant with our second child on the way. I was attempting to further my education toward my bachelor's degree, was in the process of building our first home, and was working extra jobs because money was tight. My responsibilities in the department were increasing and I felt like I was being pulled in every direction. Mentally and physically, I was exhausted and just when I thought it couldn't get worse, it did.

While my wife was getting ready to deliver our baby in a few months, my son Christopher started to get sick. He was a normal active toddler who was always happy, with a perpetual smile on his face. He rarely complained about anything, but started to show signs of slowing down and being lethargic all the time, often sleeping for most of the day. He complained about his legs and arms hurting and was having difficulty walking, although he was used to running around. We decided to have him seen by his pediatrician. Chris was originally diagnosed with an upper respiratory infection, but because he was so lethargic, the doctor wanted some additional bloodwork done, suspecting it might be anemia. Over the next few days, we anxiously awaited the results. While having dinner a few nights later, we received a phone call from the doctor, who said that the results were back. He informed me that the tests indicated Chris had acute lymphatic leukemia.

Hearing those words, I felt as if someone had just stabbed me in the heart. I then had to break the news to my wife, along with my parents and in-laws. The doctor did his best to reassure me that this wasn't a death sentence. There were many new drugs being used and their results were promising. He set up an appointment for us to see his personal friend, who was in charge of pediatric oncology at Beth Israel Hospital in New York City. We arrived the next day at the hospital and the diagnosis was confirmed. This began a seven-year journey of driving back and forth into the city for treatments and observations and Chris was admitted into the hospital for approximately four weeks. I was donating blood and platelets as often as possible and my fellow officers donated on a regular basis. I used up all my vacation time to be by my son's side. He was so young and scared and it broke my heart that this little boy had to endure so much trauma.

Three months later, my second son Michael was born. It felt good to be happy for a while with the joy of having a healthy new son. On the other hand, my marriage had deteriorated. It was hard to work on our issues as a couple with a newborn son at home and every second of every day spent on keeping my other son alive. I spent many hours each day asking God why this happened and how could he let this happen to a sweet and innocent child. I begged for answers. Christopher's first year of treatment was the most difficult, but weekly visits to the city turned into biweekly visits which eventually turned into monthly visits. As the years went on, his health improved, but there was always that thought of how long it would last and if there would be a day when they could no longer help my son.

Seven years passed and the mental strain had taken its toll on me, both physically and emotionally. I was truly at my wits' end and still begging for God's answer as to why. I was working the midnight shift one night in December during a blizzard. It had been snowing all week, the temperature was in the low teens, there were about two feet of snow on the ground, and the winds were swirling, causing massive snow drifts. I pulled into the parking lot of my church to ask God one last time, "Why?" It was 3:00 am and I had been crying for about an hour. There wasn't a soul on the road and there was almost zero visibility. I put my face in my hands, leaning on the steering wheel while I contemplated doing the unthinkable. My anger at God was so intense and so irrational that all I wanted to do was to take out my frustrations by unhooking my shotgun from the rack in my car, enter the church, and start shooting in hopes of killing God.

With the shotgun resting in my lap and considering this obviously ridiculous plan that stemmed from my depression, I heard a tapping on my driver's side window. At first I thought I imagined it, because no one in their right mind would be out in a blizzard, but then I heard it again. Rolling down my window, I saw the figure of a man standing next to my car. Initially, I didn't recognize him because he was covered from head to toe in snow. It wasn't until I heard him speak, with his familiar Irish brogue, that I knew it was Father Mike, my pastor and friend. His first words to me were, "Is everything okay? Are you alright?" Wiping the tears from my eyes and hardly able to say a word, I whispered, "No."

He asked if he could sit with me in the car. I agreed to let him in and asked, "What are you doing here?" He told me that he was sleeping in his bed at the rectory, which was right across the street, when he was awakened by a voice or spirit that told him, "Go to the church. You are needed there." Being a man of God, he didn't hesitate for a minute. He believed his presence was needed, so he left the comfort of his warm bed, got dressed, walked about one hundred yards in a blizzard, and found me in my car. Now, I had had many conversations before with Father Mike regarding my son's situation, but he always told me to have faith and that God was always listening. As I spoke with him over the course of four hours, I admitted that I thought I was losing my faith and didn't know how much more of this I could take. He placed his hand on my shoulder, gazed directly into my eyes, and assured me, "Your faith is strong. Don't give up on God. He hears you."

By the end of our long discussion, the blizzard had subsided, the sun was rising, and I asked if I could drive him home. He insisted it wasn't necessary and that the walk would do him good, and said he would remember me and my family at the mass on Sunday.

A few days later was Christopher's regular checkup in New York. He was in great spirits as I drove him in. I parked the car and held his hand as we walked to our appointment, with his mother and brother in tow. As usual, the doctor arrived, was very cordial, and asked my son how he was doing. Chris only responded, "No needles today, right?" The doctor said it was a routine checkup, encouraged him to take his pick of the lollipops, and they walked off together. I didn't know why, but I had a strange feeling that for some reason this was going to be the day we would be told that there was nothing more they could do for him. As I anxiously waited for them to return, my wife sat in one chair with her eyes closed and silently prayed while I kept my son Mike, who was then seven, occupied in the corner of the room with coloring books and toys. The door finally opened and standing in the doorway was the doctor, holding Christopher's hand.

Normally, the doctor would just say that he

was good, but instead he walked Chris over and sat in the chair next to me. Seeing this, my heart fell because I thought I was going to hear my worst fears come true. The doctor wore an expression I had never seen before. At last he spoke, saying, "I don't know how to explain this, but the lab work indicates that they could not find one leukemic cell in his blood." I was speechless and asked if he was sure Chris really had leukemia. The doctor just smiled and stated that he was my son's doctor for seven years and knew for a fact that Chris definitely did. He added that he wanted to double-check his findings and immediately send my son to Mount Sinai Hospital. We took him right away, even though Chris made a fuss about not wanting to go, but I promised him a trip to McDonald's afterward. While at Mount Sinai, all the results were confirmed. Chris was considered to be in deep remission, with no trace of leukemia in his body. We were advised to follow up yearly until we were told otherwise. We immediately left for McDonald's, where Chris devoured two cheeseburgers, french fries, and a chocolate shake. Staring at him across the table, I was in disbelief from what I had just been told. My son looked so happy. Then Father Mike's words hit me like a lightning bolt: "Your faith is strong. Don't give up on God. He hears you."

Since that incident in the church parking lot, I have never lost faith again. I know my God hears my prayers. I believe the healing of my son was a true miracle and that God has continued to bless me and look out for me throughout my years both on and off the job. My son Chris is now in his forties. He is healthy, married, and a police officer in the same department in which I served.

CHAPTER 21
PROM NIGHT HUMOR

We received a directive from the chief, who wanted us to be aware that it was Senior Prom Week and there would be a lot of parties. He wanted us to be sure that the safety of the students was primary. It was also evaluation week for my probation officers. Customarily, I would ride along and evaluate the progress of the new officers. For example, once they left the building I would observe how they visually inspected their patrol vehicles. They were to check the interior for hidden contraband that might have been left from previous arrests. In addition, they were supposed to check that the radio was working correctly and that the lights and sirens were properly functioning. As far as the exterior was concerned, they were looking for any signs of physical damage since they were responsible for the vehicle during their shift. Once on the road, I would observe how they handled the operation of their patrol car. Finally, I would evaluate how they handled the calls assigned to them and mostly how they interacted with the public. On this night, I would let them handle all calls without inter-ference and then critique their actions later.

I had done this many times before and found it to be a great training tool. The officer I was riding with on this particular night was Officer Steve Rizzo. He was about six feet tall with short blonde hair. He weighed about one hundred and eighty pounds and wore glasses. He was nervous that night because he knew he was being evaluated. He came from a po-lice family and I'm sure there was a lot of pressure put on him to follow in the footsteps of his brothers and uncles. I noticed while we were driving that he had a death grip on the steering wheel. He stared straight ahead, not wanting to take his eyes off the road. I had told him to relax and that this was not going to be a graded ride-along. I was there to help him in any way I could to make him a more competent officer.

As the night progressed, there were many calls, but this was normal for the 7:00 pm to 3:00 am tour. Rizzo was just starting to relax when we received a 10-15 call at 11:30 pm, which was an accident with injuries. A second patrol car was dispatched due to multiple phone calls about a van that was upside down, with people trapped inside. Arriving on scene, the first thing I noticed was that there were three cars and one van involved in the accident. Two cars were off the road with slight damage and people were standing outside of the vehicles. The third car, with considerable damage to the passenger side, was alongside the van. The driver was still in that car. He had a minor head injury and it was not life-threatening. As Rizzo and I approached the van that lay upside down, I could see the windows were either broken or missing and there were screams coming from the passengers inside. Officer Rizzo got down on the ground and crawled into the van. Within seconds, he reappeared. His face was white, his hands were shaking, and he claimed to be covered in blood and body parts. He looked at me and said, "I can't go back in there. It's a mess. I think I'm going to vomit." With that, he stepped aside so he could compose himself. I could still hear people calling for help, so I got down on the ground and began to crawl inside the van. With my flashlight on, I found four teenagers; two boys and two girls. They were all dressed up in formal attire and appeared to be coming from a prom. From what I could see, it looked like a war zone, with their clothes stained in what appeared to be blood. I asked, "Is anyone hurt?" To my surprise, they all said no but screamed, "Please get us out of here!" One by one, I led them by the hand to the window where I had entered and each one was successfully able to crawl to safety.

Officer Maguire was in the second patrol car that responded to the accident. From inside, I could hear him call out, "Sarge, are you alright in there?" When he did not hear my immediate response, he quickly got on the ground and crawled into the van to check on me. Now that both of us were in the vehicle, we were able to scan the interior with more light. We didn't locate any more passengers, but we were able to see that some type of substance was dripping from the walls. It had a familiar smell, but I couldn't put my finger on it. All of a sudden, Officer Maguire noticed four large shallow white boxes in the rear of the van and burst out laughing. He grinned to me, "Oh, my God. I think I just solved the mystery of blood and body parts." Apparently, after the prom was over, the teenagers went to get pizza and soda for themselves and some other friends. When the accident occurred and the van flipped, the pizzas went flying out of their boxes and splattered all over the interior of the vehicle. The soda containers also burst, leaving the van and the teens covered in foaming cherry soda. The goo that Rizzo believed was body parts and blood was actually sausage, cheese, and pepperoni pizza toppings combined with the cherry soda.

Now, Maguire was the prankster of the squad and wasn't about to let this rookie go without being taught a lesson. He begged me to let Rizzo know the final outcome, yet he still wanted to have some fun with it. I told him that he could, but not to go too far. As I climbed out of the van, I called Rizzo over. He looked like death warmed over and asked, "What did you find in there, Sarge?" I told him that Maguire was bringing out something and needed his assistance. With that, Maguire crawled out with a handful of goop and commented, "It's not bad and it's still warm. Do you want a taste?" Rizzo's knees started to buckle and his eyes began to roll back in his head as if he were about to faint. I quickly grabbed him and sat him down on the curb. Maguire, still eating the handful of pizza, chuckled, "Welcome to the squad, rookie. Next time you bring the pizza." The lightbulb went on as Rizzo finally realized that what he thought was blood and body parts was in reality pizza and soda. Of course, the lesson I tried to teach him was that you should always think before speaking or reacting, because you will be judged by your actions.

CHAPTER 22
THE CAVE-IN RESCUE

I would routinely meet with my second-in-command and discuss the progress of our probation officers. One such meeting nearly turned deadly. After assigning sectors and doing a weapons check, I took my second, Officer Joe Morris, aside and advised him that he was going to be my driver for the shift. This time together was going to include a discussion and progress report of the "probies." Before going on the road, I had Joe pull the evaluation folders of all the new officers. Once a month, I would prepare reports on various weaknesses and strengths and how we were addressing their progress. This report went to the division commander and then on to the chief. As we were going over the reports, we received a message from the traffic and safety road sergeant. He advised me that he needed

assistance in an area where there was construction for a water main being dug along the
side of Crestview Drive. Traffic was being im-
paired by the heavy equipment blocking the
roadway, causing a lot of congestion. His unit
was running radar across town and his manpower was low, so I told him I would check on
it the first chance I got.

Officer Morris and I had been working the
morning shift, which ran from 8:00 am to
4:00 pm, when the traffic and safety sergeant
called. It was 10:00 am when we arrived at
the construction site and we found that the
complaints were legitimate. We saw heavy
dump trucks and excavating equipment on the
shoulder of the road that, along with numerous
workers, were blocking part of the paved road.
I asked to speak to the foreman or supervisor
in charge, but the workers did not understand
English very well. I was eventually directed
to Mr. Ed Lally, site supervisor, and informed
him about our concerns regarding the traffic
problem he was creating. I told him he needed
to move his equipment over to a grassy area
because it was impeding traffic and vehicles
could not pass safely. As we spoke, I heard a
lot of commotion in the area where his men
were digging the trench for the water line and
noticed that there were few safety barriers in

place. I also saw men working without hard hats or safety belts. The walls of the trench appeared unstable because there was sand slowly sliding into the trench. I informed Lally that these issues needed to be addressed immediately; otherwise, I would shut down the project. He simply replied that they were way behind schedule due to all the recent rain. Just then, Officer Morris approached to tell me that headquarters was calling and we were needed there. Before we left, I warned Lally that I would be checking up on him and to fix the problems.

Officer Morris and I had barely gotten two blocks away when the call came in that there was a cave-in at the construction site, with injuries. We turned around and responded with our lights and sirens on. Once we arrived, Joe jumped out of the car, popped the trunk, and retrieved his oxygen unit and first aid kit. Looking into the trench, which was about ten to fifteen feet deep, he could see three men. One was buried up to his chest in dirt and screaming for help while the other two tried to dig him out. Joe ordered them out because he could see that the dirt was so tightly packed around the trapped man's torso, it was causing him to hyperventilate. Joe then jumped into the hole and tried to remove the dirt from around the man's chest with his hands, hoping he could relieve some of the pressure that was squeezing him. Unfortunately, this wasn't working. As he removed dirt, more would slide in from the collapsing sides.

By this time, I had reached the trench and grabbed Joe's oxygen unit, which he had left on the ground, in case we needed to get it to the man. Just then, the ground grumbled and the sides of the trench began to cave in. Joe was still digging with his hands and paying no attention to the collapsing walls because he was so focused on saving the worker. Little by little, the man was being buried deeper. His face was almost completely covered in dirt but Joe, with his other hand, kept trying to keep it cleared so he could breathe. As the collapse continued, Joe found himself buried to the middle of his thighs and I jumped in to help. I still had the oxygen unit on me, so I gave it to Joe and instructed him to put it on the man's face. As he did, more dirt poured into the hole, leaving the man totally submerged and Joe buried up to his chest. I ordered the other workers to get plywood and lumber to support the walls. I wasn't sure if the trapped man was even alive, but I knew I had to get Morris out before he was completely covered. One of the workers threw a small shovel into the hole and I began digging furiously. I was able to get one of Joe's arms free and he instructed me to dig down along his other arm because his hand was still holding the oxygen mask on the man's face. I was eventually able to see the top of the trapped worker's head and we continued digging until we could clear the dirt away from his face. He was still receiving oxygen and he was blinking, so we knew he was alive. As the plywood was lowered into the hole and propped against the sides, the reinforcement was working and the dirt slowly stopped. With the trench stable, more men were able to jump into the hole to continue digging. The foreman moved his backhoe as close as he could without causing any more cave-ins and stretched the arm of his equipment over the trench. At the end of his bucket, he made a makeshift sling and was able to get it around Joe's body, freeing him from the hole. The other workers and I continued to clear more dirt away from the man and removed the oxygen mask to see if he was responsive. He was, so we got the bucket with the sling back again and wrapped it around his waist and chest, gradually lifting him out.

Fortunately, Officer Morris had no injuries. The other man was taken to the hospital with two broken legs and a fractured pelvis. His recovery was made possible thanks to the heroic efforts of Officer Joe Morris.

The next day, I requested that Officer Morris receive the Life Saving Award and recommended that he receive the Police Star for bravery. Through his extraordinary efforts, with total disregard for his own life, he was able to jump into a collapsing trench, remove dirt away from a trapped man, and maintain an oxygen flow to someone who was virtually being buried alive. The Police Star was our department's second highest award. Had Joe perished during the rescue, he no doubt would have posthumously received our department's highest award, the Medal of Honor. I thank God that didn't happen. It was decided that Officer Morris would receive both of the recommended awards and that I would receive the Lifesaving Award, along with the Departmental Citation for Excellence, because of my role in the incident.

CHAPTER 23
DAVID WEINBERG

One day, about a week after the cave-in incident, I was sitting at my desk at work. It was just one of those days where my head felt like it was about to explode from stress and having to deal with piles of paperwork. On days like this, I would take a drive to clear my head, keep me centered, and free my mind of the paperwork. I decided that instead of taking my usual patrol car, I would take the Chevy Suburban. It was a huge SUV and built like a tank. It had all types of equipment and soaked up gas like a sponge, but it was fun to drive and had plenty of leg room. Walking to the parking lot, I ran into Officer Morris, who had just gotten out of court. He glanced at me and asked, "Do you want some company? You look like you need it." I gave him an affirming nod and he slid into the passenger seat.

We drove for a few minutes, discussing the previous week's cave-in and how lucky we were that no one died, then decided to pull into the local diner and pick up two coffees to go. We were sitting in the parking lot and enjoying our coffee when we noticed a station wagon traveling northbound on Highway 65 and moving toward us. There was heavy smoke billowing out of the rear of the car. Clearly, any car traveling behind it was visually affected, so we had no choice but to stop this wreck of a vehicle before someone got hurt. As the car went by, we pulled out and put on our red lights to try to pull him over. Because there was so much smoke, the driver couldn't see the lights, so we had to turn on our sirens. Finally, he pulled over to the shoulder of the road. Over my PA system, I advised him to turn off the vehicle and once he did, I walked over. Before I could reach him, his door opened and he stepped out.

As he exited his vehicle, I saw a man that could only be described as a smaller Danny DeVito. This gentleman stood no more than 4'5" at best. He appeared to be in his mid to late forties, wore black-rimmed glasses, a tattered sport coat, and sneakers, and had only a small amount of hair on either side of his otherwise bald head. I asked for his license, registration, and insurance card and he informed me that they were in the car, which belonged to his sister. I instructed him to retrieve the documents and bring them to me in the Suburban. While I waited, I ran his plate number to be sure the car wasn't stolen, but it came back clean.

Officer Morris had been laughing hysterically at the sight of me standing next to the driver because we looked like David and Goliath. Remember, I stood at about 6'3" and weighed around two hundred and fifty pounds. The man, in turn, was about two feet smaller and at least a hundred to a hundred fifty pounds lighter. Joe just chuckled, "Oh, my God. Please, just give him a warning and send him on his way. I can't take any more of this." Of course, I thought this was an extreme safety issue and that it would be irresponsible to not address this problem immediately.

The driver got out of his car and headed toward me, waving his credentials. I rolled down the window and this little hand reached in with his paperwork. Then his other hand reached up and he grabbed the edge of the window with these little short stubby fingers. The Suburban sat high off the ground due to its heavy suspension and bigger wheels. Most average size people would not have a hard time looking into the vehicle, but this gentleman was certainly having a hard time because I could barely see the top of his head. He was trying to pull himself up so he could speak with me face to face. With a strong ethnic New York accent, he said, "Officer. Officer. Officer, I was in a hurry and I didn't mean to speed..." I interrupted him in mid-sentence and told him he wasn't stopped for speeding; he was being pulled over because his car was a hazard on the road due to all of the smoke coming out of the rear. After a brief pause, still dangling from the window with his little sneakers banging on my car door for leverage, he asked, "Officer, is it possible that you could give me a break?" By this time, Officer Morris was speechless and practically wetting his pants. He was laughing so hard that our Suburban was starting to shake. He kept glancing out his side of the vehicle, not wanting to make eye contact with little David Weinberg, as his name appeared on the paperwork. Not wanting Joe to fall out of the car, I agreed to let the man go with a warning, with the understanding that he would get the car repaired as soon as possible. He hopped off of my vehicle and returned to his car. About halfway there, he turned with a broad smile, holding his papers in his tiny little left hand.

With his right hand, he pointed at me and said, "Officer, you're a real saint. A real saint, I tell you. Thank you, thank you, thank you."

As the man drove away in a cloud of smoke, Joe and I exchanged glances and started cracking up, laughing like school kids playing during recess. That car stop temporarily relieved all the stress I was carrying when I started out the day. Thank you, little David. I may have made your day, but you certainly made mine, also.

CHAPTER 24
THE PRINCIPAL'S OFFICE

I had been in the police department for more than ten years and believed that I was well-prepared and trained to handle a multitude of situations. I was supervising many men, handling investigations, making sure that rules and regulations were being followed with the department, and protecting and serving our town.

I was the father of two sons who were as different as night and day. My older boy was eight and in the second grade and my younger son was in kindergarten. I had enrolled them in a Catholic elementary school because I thought they would do well with structure and discipline. This held true for my firstborn, who was a model student. He would leave the house every morning impeccably dressed in his school uniform, wearing his navy blue pants, a powder blue collared shirt, a school tie, and black shiny dress shoes. All he would have needed was the New York Times newspaper rolled up under his arm and you would swear you were looking at a banker. Every day when I picked him up at 3:30 pm, he looked exactly the same as when he left in the morning. My younger son, on the other hand, was a different story. He was six years old and had this beautiful, angelic face. He was a very smart boy with an inquisitive mind who always asked questions and wanted to know how and why things worked. However, although he left for school dressed just like his brother, he never looked the same at the end of the day when he was picked up. He always appeared as if he had been mugged. His shirt was never tucked in his pants, there were usually one or two buttons missing off of his shirt, his pants were filthy, and those black shoes that started off shiny were usually covered in dirt. Sometimes he even came home without his tie and, when questioned about its whereabouts, he never knew. I thought I should probably start buying his ties in bulk.

One day while sitting at my desk, my secretary advised me that the school principal wanted to see me. My first thought was, "Are my children alright?" She told me they were both fine and it was in reference to my younger son, Michael. I knew right then and there that this was not going to be good. I immediately left work and drove to my son's school, where I was directed to the principal's office. Michael was sitting outside, looking just as disheveled as he did at the end of every school day. Seeing me, he gave me that bright angelic smile, which I knew meant trouble. I asked him why we were there. He leaned in close to me and softly whispered, "I don't know. I did what they told me to do." I told him to stay seated while I met with the principal, Sister Madeline, in her office. His teacher, Mrs. Fisher, was also present. The conversation that transpired left me speechless.

Mrs. Fisher informed me that Michael was being his usual disruptive self in class by talking and making the other kids laugh. After she asked him four times to stop, he left her no choice but to give him a time out and put him in the closet located in the back of the room. The closet was spacious, similar to a large walk-in closet in a house. It held the children's jackets, lunches, art supplies etc. and there was even a chair to sit on, along with a light switch, so he wouldn't be sitting in the dark. I found out that the chair was commonly referred to as "Michael's Chair." Hearing this, I was outraged that the only way of disciplining my son was to put him on a chair in the closet. Before I could say a word, the principal said that this wasn't an unusual punishment and that other students were sent to the same time-out chair when disruptive. While I was still reeling from the thought that my six-year-old was put in a closet, Mrs. Fisher continued, "Maybe you should hear why you are here." I suggested that she bring my son into the office with us so he could be a part of this conversation. He entered the room like a happy-go-lucky boy, smiling at everyone and looking as if he didn't have a care in the world. That's when his teacher dropped the hammer as to why I was really there. She informed me that while he was in the closet, she heard him singing and talking to himself, with rustling sounds that she couldn't quite figure out. There was then a long period of silence that made her nervous and prompted her to check in on him. Upon opening the closet door, to her horror, she found him sitting in his chair eating all of the students' lunches. With an exasperated look, she turned to me and said, "Well?"

Fighting every impulse in my body not to laugh hysterically, I covered my mouth with my hand, removed my glasses, and turned to

Michael. Without hesitation, he pointed at Mrs. Fisher and said, "What? She put me in there!" I then asked him why he ate his friends' lunches. As innocently as only a six-year-old could, he replied, "I was hungry." I told him he couldn't possibly eat twenty lunches and he explained, "I was looking for one that I liked." Apparently, he would take a bite out of a random sandwich and if he didn't like it, he would put it back and go on to the next one. He continued this until his stomach felt full.

After hearing what had happened, I could no longer be upset about Michael being put in the closet. I turned to Mrs. Fisher, who seemed totally frustrated, and apologized profusely for my son's behavior. I then looked at Sister Madeline, who had her hand over her mouth. I could see that she saw the humor in this story and was holding back a smile. I'm sure I even saw a few suppressed tears of laughter in her eyes. She asked me, "How are we going to make this situation right?" After a short pause, I assured her I would take care of the situation by speaking with Michael privately and bringing in lunches for all of the students the next day in hopes that it would never happen again. This would become just one of many trips to visit with Sister Madeline.

I recall receiving another phone call at work a few months later, once again requesting my presence at school. It seemed that Michael was at it again and Mrs. Fisher was beside herself. As I entered the building, there was my son, sitting in his usual spot on the bench right outside the principal's office. I glanced at him and he gave me a shoulder shrug before I went inside to meet with the principal and Mrs. Fisher and be advised of his latest escapade. Evidently, Michael's classmate and best friend, Roger, was having a birthday and his mother, Mrs. Moger, had brought into school a tray of twenty-four chocolate-covered cupcakes to share with his class. They were placed on a table in the back of the room. All the kids were excited about celebrating Roger's birthday and eating a snack during break. When the time came, Roger was asked to go to the back of the room and bring his tray up to the front of the class, where they would all sing to him and make a fuss. Making his way up the aisle, he could hear his classmates cheering, clapping, and wishing him a happy birthday. As he passed each row of students, they would turn around to see the delicious treats they would soon be eating. While approaching Michael's desk, he somehow got his feet tangled with my son's, causing him to trip, topple the tray, and fall facedown into the chocolate-covered

cupcakes. Of course, the entire class erupt-
ed into uncontrollable laughter, with Michael
laughing the loudest. When the teacher saw
Roger covered in cupcakes on his face, in his
hair, and all over his shirt, looking humiliated
and embarrassed, Michael's loud laughter was
the straw that broke the camel's back. She
could only assume that he had intentionally
stuck out his foot so Roger would fall, so she
immediately grabbed Michael by the back of
his shirt collar and personally escorted him to
the principal.

In the office, these circumstances were relayed to me. I found it hard to believe for a
couple of reasons. First of all, Roger was my
son's best friend and Michael would never intentionally hurt him. Secondly, there was going to be a birthday celebration where food
was involved. Chocolate-covered cupcakes
were Michael's favorite and he would never
do anything to jeopardize getting that treat.
I asked him, in front of the teacher and principal, to tell me his side of the story. As mischievous as he was, he was never one to lie
to me and he explained, "I was just trying to
get a good look at the cupcakes when Roger
passed by. I would never try to trip him! It was
an accident." Mrs. Fisher was obviously not
buying one word of it. She pointed at Michael

and started shrieking, "He is the devil's spawn and I'm at my wits' end!" Before I could say a word, Sister Madeline told her, "There are no devils that live in this school; just loving little children." I believed my son when he said it wasn't intentional, but it was his word against the teacher's and nothing was going to be resolved. It was an unfortunate accident and although Michael's feet did get tangled with Roger's, I felt he shared some responsibility and wanted to make it right. I suggested to Sister Madeline that I would bring in a new batch of cupcakes the next morning to make up for that day's mishap. She thankfully accepted my offer. The following day, I showed up with a few trays of cupcakes from the local bakery and Roger got his class birthday celebration without incident. Michael even made him a homemade birthday card.

I could see how Mrs. Fisher might think the worst of Michael, based upon his past behavior in class, but the truth was that he was a smart and curious little boy. He was happy and playful and always told me the truth. As he grew up, he never lost his thirst for knowledge and continued to ask the question, "Why?" He finished his elementary education at that same school, thanks to the patience of Sister Madeline and all of his other teachers. Throughout high school and college, Michael maintained high academic grades and became an outstanding athlete who was scouted by four Major League Baseball teams. The ironic part in all of this is that he received his college degree in education, although he ultimately decided to follow in my footsteps and joined law enforcement. He is now a top-rated detective in my old department and is married with three children of his own.

CHAPTER 25
MY SON'S TENTH BIRTHDAY

There is an old saying that goes, "I just happened to be in the right place at the right time." Well, there is also another saying that goes, "I just happened to be in the wrong place at the wrong time." The latter of the two was how I felt this one particular night. My squad was working the 4:00 pm to 12:00 midnight shift on the north side of town. It had been an extremely busy day and we were working with minimum manpower because some men were out sick or on vacation. Since this was one of the busiest shifts, we never should have been understaffed with officers on the road. I had requested that the watch commander call the midnight shift in early, but my request was denied. When we were this short-staffed, it meant that most calls would be handled by one car with only one patrolman. There wouldn't be backup and this could lead to extremely dangerous situations. As a sergeant and road supervisor with new young officers on my squad, I routinely would check on them by responding to their calls in case they needed backup. Because this night had been so busy and all the sector cars couldn't keep up as they were inundated with calls, I ended up handling some of them myself.

As mentioned earlier, one of the most dangerous calls you could go on was a domestic disturbance. Dispatch had radioed in to the Sector 2 car, which was operated by one of the newer officers, to respond to a domestic call. A husband and wife were arguing and injuries were reported. Since the sector car was held up on a previous call for a bank escort, I thought I should respond and, due to his lack of experience, I wanted to back him up should he get there before me. By then, dispatch was receiving more calls about a woman banging on apartment doors and screaming and that she was covered in blood. I advised dispatch that I was responding because the Sector 2 car was just finishing up elsewhere and I was the closest car. I also remembered that it was my younger son's tenth birthday and I had been hoping to stop in at his birthday dinner during my break. I figured that I was going to be late or might not get there at all.

Arriving on the scene, I was approached by a bloodied woman who spoke very little broken English. She was pointing toward apartment 10B, which happened to be a downstairs unit. All of the interior lights were out, so it was dark with the exception of the porch light. The interior door was open, but the screen door was closed. The neighbor who had initially called the police then arrived. She was Russian and had spoken to the victim. She told me that the woman had been beaten by her husband many times, but that day had been the worst. She informed me that he was home and in the apartment, but to be careful because he had a very bad temper. Taking note of this information, I asked if there were any weapons in the residence. The neighbor didn't know but said she would ask the wife, who was sitting on the front lawn, holding her head. I radioed headquarters and called for an ambulance.

By that time, Officer Bob Walker had arrived and I advised him of the situation. He administered some first aid to her until the ambulance arrived. Still not knowing whether there were weapons inside, we both walked toward the apartment and stood outside on the step. I called through the door, identified myself as a police officer, and asked if the man inside would please step out so we could discuss what happened. There was no response. We cautiously reached for the door, aware of the possible violent nature of the husband. Suddenly, the screen door violently flew open, just missing me and causing Walker to take a few steps back to avoid being hit. The husband started yelling something in Russian, which I didn't understand, and stepped forward with a gun in his hand, pointed directly at me. I recognized that it was a forty-five automatic. He was about three feet away and his finger was on the trigger, ready to fire. Instinctively, I reached out to deflect his gun. At the same time, I pulled out my gun and Walker stepped forward, striking the man in the face with his nightstick. He instantly fell to the ground and dropped the gun, so I reholstered by weapon once I realized that the imminent danger of being shot was gone. I easily could have shot him and would have been within my rights, had Walker not intervened.

Two more patrol cars arrived and assisted Walker with the arrest. Both the husband and wife were treated for injuries and taken to a nearby hospital. I bent over the step where the gun was still laying, picked it up, and noticed that the slide was jammed open. When the guy loaded his clip in the dark, it didn't load properly, causing the gun to jam. If it hadn't, I most certainly would have been shot dead. As I held the gun, Officer Walker headed over, looked at it, and commented, "Christ, Sarge. You are one lucky bastard. You should be dead. At that range, he couldn't possibly have missed." I merely nodded. I could hardly speak because it had happened so quickly, but I managed to thank Walker for covering my back.

As the scene cleared out and the patrol cars went back on the road, I sat quietly in my car and reflected on what had taken place. I really couldn't have done anything differently other than to "always expect the unexpected." Once again, my guardian angel was looking over me and remaining by my side. Had he not been there, my son would have always remembered that his father died on his tenth birthday. I thank the good Lord every day for watching over me and keeping me safe.

CHAPTER 26
RICK'S BAR

A few days after the domestic violence incident involving the Russian, I was having lunch with Sal Alfano. He was telling me about a special detail that the chief was forming. Alfano was working out of the division commander's office and would be doing the scheduling, and wanted to give me a heads up in case I was interested. He said his boss was getting plenty of heat from the chief about the bars and social clubs in town. They were getting numerous complaints from neighbors regarding public lewdness, urinating on the sidewalks, foul language, and fighting, and the chief wanted it stopped.

There was going to be a posting for three sergeants and eighteen officers to work a new shift. This shift was going to be from 7:00 pm to 3:00 am and broken up into three squads, each consisting of one sergeant and six officers. The squads' schedules would overlap, putting two sergeants and twelve officers on the streets at one time to supplement and assist the regularly scheduled sector cars' calls. This would ensure that there would no longer be manpower shortages during high peak times. By the end of the week, the chief had picked his detail and I had the good fortune to be chosen as one of the sergeants. I was a little concerned about who the other sergeants would be because I wanted true professionals that would go the extra mile, not ones that were just putting in their time. That worry was put to rest when I was told the names of the other two. The first one was Ted Roland. He was about 5'10" tall and in his early thirties. He was well built, experienced, and very progressive – always willing to try something new. He ran a good squad and his men respected him. The second was Don Fisher. He was the elder statesman of the crew, straight-laced, and would bend the rules if needed, but always respected the law. He was tough as nails and someone you wouldn't want to anger, and he always stuck up for his men. Being the youngest of the three, I knew I would learn and benefit from their experience. There were times that I objected strongly on certain issues regarding procedure, but we would always find a way to talk it out and resolve our differences.

One night while I was working, I called a meeting of the sergeants to discuss a procedural problem having to do with taking patrol cars off the road during night court. It seemed to me that taking the men off the road to appear in court was defeating the purpose of the new shifts that were formed. After much discussion, we decided that the nighttime court cases would be changed to days, leaving the power shift intact. The officers could go to court in the daytime, get paid overtime for their court appearance, and would be back on the road for their shift, thus not jeopardizing the public safety of our town's residents.

A week or so later, while working, we received a call that Rick's Bar was getting out of control. Let me tell you a little about this place. To call it a dive would be kind. As you pulled up to this bar, you immediately felt like you needed a tetanus shot. Located off Highway 510, it was a two-story building with cracked steps leading to the entrance. Some of the windows were painted black so you couldn't see inside and the gray exterior paint of the building was chipped and peeling off. The parking lot was made of dirt and rocks, not paved. You automatically thought it should be condemned once you saw it. The florescent sign outside the building read Rick's Bar in flashing red lights, except the "R" had been burnt out for years, so the sign just read "ick's Bar" – a perfect name for it.

The owner, Rick Cicone, was a true lowlife. He catered to the worst of the worst. He was a short guy with a beer belly in his early sixties. He wore glasses that were always held together with tape and gave the impression that he lived on the streets because he looked like a bum and was always disheveled. He smoked cheap cigars and the stench of them stayed with him. His shirts usually had burn holes in them from the falling ashes. He was arrogant and had a nasty attitude. He hated the cops because months earlier, I was asked to meet the ABC (Alcohol Beverage Control) inspector at the bar for a routine check. ABC found multiple violations, including the watering down or diluting of liquor, failure to post the bar's license, and removing the labels off some bottles and replacing them with different labels from more expensive brands to overcharge the customers. This yielded him multiple hefty fines and he was forced to close the bar for a week. All of this came on the heels of the town's building and health inspectors and fire marshals citing him for a multitude of violations.

On any given night, you would find drug dealers, wannabe bikers, local lowlifes, prostitutes, and an assortment of dirtbags in the bar. This mixed crowd was an accident waiting to happen and this was going to be the night. The drinking and partying had been going on all day. Different groups of people had been there for hours and were getting extremely drunk and out of control. Apparently, one of the bikers made a very unkind sexual slur toward one of the local girls, who was the girlfriend of Seth Greenbush. The Greenbush family lived right across the street from Rick's Bar on a double lot of land that was almost an acre. Their house faced the side of the bar. This family could only be described as transplanted hillbillies from the Ozarks. There were fifteen family members, all adults, living in the house along with their dogs. The yard was filled with junk cars, debris, car parts, tires, and even a boat with a hole in its side. The house itself seemed to be in the same condition as the bar, a true eyesore.

Seth was in the bar, heard the sexual slur about his girlfriend, and became enraged. He had to defend the honor of his woman, so he spit in the biker's face and all hell broke loose.

Somehow, word got back to the Greenbush family that Seth was getting the crap kicked out of him. All the family members, including the dogs, ran across the street and into the bar. From that point on, it was a true Old West barroom brawl. Everyone was punching everyone else and the dogs were attacking and biting anyone that got near them. Half of the crowd was fighting inside the bar while the other half took the brawl outside to the street. This was when the dispatch phone lines lit up like a Christmas tree. One caller said there were about a hundred people fighting, when in reality it was probably half that amount but they were loud, noisy, and out of control. Dispatch sent both sector cars, along with the special detail, just to be sure. Two sergeants and fourteen officers responded to the scene.

By the time we all arrived, the brawl was at its peak. It was sheer chaos. Almost half of the people involved were members of the Greenbush family, including women that were not afraid to throw punches. Now, the Greenbush family was notorious for fighting with cops and any other authoritative figures. They really thought that they were above the law. I had dealt with them a few times, so I knew what to expect. They stuck together, so if you fought with one of them, you ended up fighting with all of them. As we were trying to break up the fighting and regain some semblance of order, one of my officers got struck in the head with a pool stick, causing him to go down. We cops stick together, as well, so if you go after one of us, you're going to get all of us. That was when it got personal. While trying to attend to my officer's wounds, I saw Mark Greenbush, one of the brothers, and a biker going after each other with baseball bats. Three of my officers got involved in their brawl and knocked them out cold with their nightsticks before rolling them over and handcuffing them. As I looked around again, I could see four more guys fighting and throwing chairs over each other's heads. That's when two more of my officers came flying through the front door and down the steps to subdue and handcuff them, as well. The fighting groups were getting smaller and we continued to make arrests. The body count on the ground was getting bigger and the flying objects were starting to decrease. One of the Greenbush brothers was outside by the side of the building, swinging a car bumper to try and knock people out. Two of Sergeant Fisher's men remedied the problem immediately and one more Greenbush family member was added to the pile of arrests.

When all was said and done, everyone that

had been arrested was lying on the ground and handcuffed. This included the entire Greenbush family, some bikers, local barflies, and various women. The owner, Rick Cicone, was in handcuffs and escorted out of the bar by one of my officers. He had been struck in the head with one of his own watered-down liquor bottles and was demanding medical attention and to be read his rights. He was laid on the ground alongside all the others to wait for the arrival of the multiple ambulances that had been called. Almost everyone arrested needed some sort of medical attention, as well as two officers, including the one that was hit with the pool stick and the other that got bitten by a Greenbush dog. One of the dogs died during the melee and the other was removed by the animal warden and eventually euthanized.

As a result of this particular brawl, the bar was closed pending a further investigation. Within a week, the fire company responded to a fire at Rick's Bar. By the time it was brought under control, the place was designated a total loss and never reopened again. To this day, on that very site sits Deborah's Dance Studio. The Greenbush house was eventually condemned by the building inspector and health department, and they all moved elsewhere. A beautiful two-story home now sits on that lot.

CHAPTER 27
DUGAN'S DONUTS

The police department back in the 1970s was like a big family. As in all families, you have one child who is never quite in step with the rest of the bunch. He is sometimes characterized as the "black sheep" or the problem child. Nevertheless, as a parent you still love him as much as the others, although he tries your patience at every turn. I had one such officer. His name was Bill Olsen and he reminded me of a rooster on acid. He could carry on three conversations at the same time, which made no sense to the person he was talking to, but made perfect sense to him. He was always in a hurry to go somewhere. Where, I never knew, but it was important for him to get there. As a rule, a directive or a law was always open to his interpretation in his eyes and his interpretation always turned out to be wrong. But he would do anything for you. It might not be what you wanted or needed, but he would do it anyway. He was very inquisitive and never stopped asking questions, like a child who always asks, "Why?" His intentions were pure and good-natured but his decision-making process was flawed, which led to poor choices. There is an old religious saying, "God never gives you crosses that you can't carry." When it came to Bill Olsen, my cross seemed to be extremely heavy.

I can recall one particular night when I was working the 12:00 midnight to 8:00 am tour and the shift lieutenant came to the squad room with a memo from the division commander. It stated that we should have all patrols keep a close watch on Dugan's Deli. There had been someone or something ripping open the delivery of baked goods in front of the store. Ed Dugan was a personal friend of the chief and I believe they went to school together, so priority-wise, it was put on the top of my list. Also working that particular sector that night was my black sheep, Bill Olsen. Before the officers left for their sectors, I pulled him aside and said, "Keep a close watch on Dugan's. Make sure nothing happens on our watch, got it?" He replied, "You can count on me, boss." That made me very nervous and I decided to stake out Dugan's myself. The deli was in a strip mall. It was a small place that only sat about six people at the counter along the wall, next to the register. Toward the back was the deli section, where you could purchase your favorite deli meats or pick from an assortment of baked goods such as donuts, danish, or muffins. These were not made on the premises, but brought in and delivered fresh every morning. I knew the bakery goods were usually delivered between 4:30 and 5:30 am. There was plenty of time for me to find a spot to sit and observe.

At around 4:15 am, I pulled my unmarked car into a parking lot across from Dugan's and began to wait. At 4:45 am, I noticed the sector car pulling into the parking lot. The officer got out of his car and was checking the doors making sure all was secure. He then left. I was pleasantly surprised that Olsen was doing his job so diligently by actually getting out of his car and checking the lock instead of just driving by and shining a flashlight on the door. At 5:05 am, the delivery truck arrived and placed the bakery goods by the front door, then drove away. All seemed normal except that the sector car driven by Olsen had returned. He got out of his vehicle and approached the front door. He had just been there twenty minutes before and I wondered why he was back. Within seconds, he left again. I decided to drive over to Dugan's and got out of my car to investigate. I discovered that the donut bag was ripped open and several were missing. There was a trail of powdered sugar from the bag leading to the street. I was so angry I could barely speak and could only deduce that one of two situations occurred. Either the delivery man removed some of the donuts before leaving them by the door or the unthinkable happened and Olsen was the culprit. After seeing the trail of powder, I knew my fear was correct. I radioed Olsen and told him to meet me in the parking lot of the strip mall where Dugan's was. He arrived shortly afterwards and I asked if he recalled the memo from the division commander. He nodded affirmatively. I then asked him if he recalled stating that I could count on him. He nodded his head again. Now, our uniform consisted of a black shirt, black pants, and a black tie. With Olsen standing in front of me, I could see that he was covered in white powder, so I very calmly asked him what the white powder was that was all over his shirt. I asked if it was cocaine. He was struggling for an answer to my question and I could see the wheels in his head spinning, trying to come up with an explanation. As he stared blankly into space and began stuttering, I stated,

"There can only be two possible reasons why your shirt looks the way it does. You are either a sloppy cocaine addict or you are the donut thief. Both are bad, but which is it?" He looked at me and said, "Boss, I would never do drugs."

Rubbing my eyes like a frustrated father, I asked him if he took the donuts. Looking very sheepish, he explained that usually after his shift, he stopped in at Dugan's for a coffee and got a few donuts. Ed Dugan usually comped his purchase as a courtesy. In the past weeks at about the time of delivery, he would get very hungry and since nothing was opened at that hour, he would open up the donut package and take a few. He didn't think there was anything wrong with it because he was only going to get it for free later, after his shift. I had to explain to him about the generosity of Mr. Dugan, who was giving him donuts and coffee. On the other hand, by taking it out of the package without the owner's consent, it could be described as stealing or theft. I informed him that one's generosity should never be taken for granted or be expected and told him I would never condone this type of behavior. I sternly advised Olsen that when Mr. Dugan opened up his deli at 6:30, he was going to humbly apologize and tell him that he had been opening up the packages and eating the baked goods. He would then give Dugan $20 for the items and assure him that it would never happen again. He agreed to do so.

As the tour was ending, Captain Reynolds called me into his office. He wanted to convey the compliments of the chief on a job well done in reference to the Dugan Deli problem. It seemed the chief stopped in at Ed's place for a coffee and donut before coming to work and Mr. Dugan said how pleased he was with the way his problem was handled. He wished to personally thank me and Officer Olsen for the professional manner in which everything was taken care of.

Sometimes I felt like that cross just kept getting heavier and heavier, even when it involved powdered sugar.

CHAPTER 28
THE FIRE CHIEF
VS. THE POLICE DEPARTMENT

Winter had arrived with a vengeance and it snowed almost every day. The plows just kept pushing ice and snow off the roads and onto the shoulders. The highways were becoming a mess. In the daytime, the sun would shine and cause some of the snow to melt. However, as the sun went down and the temperatures dropped, the melting snow would turn to black ice. The day shift was bad, with commuters traveling to work. The roads were full of slush and traffic congestion due to cautious drivers going slower. The night shift was a complete disaster. The plows couldn't keep up with clearing and salting the roads quickly enough. Accidents came in bunches of three, four, and five car pileups. Traffic and safety, special detail, and sector cars were all being used to handle the many accidents and they had their hands full. Nerves were becoming strained and tempers were short. We were also dealing with Christmas shoppers, office parties that involved too much merry making, and plenty of snow and ice. This was a recipe for a major problem.

I was working the 4:00 pm to 12 midnight shift on one of those bitter cold winter days when the temperature was dropping rapidly and there was still quite a bit of snow on the ground. The sector cars were dispatched to a multi-vehicle accident on our busiest highway. One of the vehicles involved was a tanker truck carrying a full load of gasoline that had jack-knifed across all three lanes, blocking traffic. Trying to avoid striking the tanker, the vehicles behind the truck were applying their brakes, causing them to slide into other cars. When I arrived, I could see that the scene was a total disaster. There were multiple collisions, with some cars on the grass divider with minor damage and others with considerable damage. There were also multiple injuries. Some people were outside the vehicles assessing their damage while other bystanders were trying to assist the injured people. I immediately requested dispatch to send for additional ambulances due to the amount of injured people, plus several tow trucks for the automobiles. As I approached the tanker, I saw that the cab's wheels were wedged underneath the side of it and several of the wheels were damaged and flat, so I knew right then and there that a heavy-duty wrecker would be needed. The driver of the tanker was uninjured and was already out of the cab when he came up to me to say that the tanker was loaded with gasoline. There was a heavy smell of fuel in the air, which concerned me because I thought that one of the sections of the tanker might have ruptured. Because this could lead to gasoline on the roadway and a possible explosion, I requested the nearest fire company to respond for a wash down to remove any gasoline from the roadway.

Little did I know that the closest company that was dispatched was in the midst of celebrating its annual Christmas party. They should have advised dispatch of their situation and had another company respond, but they didn't. A fire chief and eight firefighters arrived at the accident, all of whom had a little too much Christmas spirit. It was obvious that they had all been drinking. A confrontation broke out between the police officers and the firefighters as to who was in charge of the scene. I forcefully told the chief that

I wanted to move the tanker truck to a side road and get it off the major roadway due to the potential danger of an explosion. The fire chief stepped in front of the truck where I was standing, grabbed me by the jacket, and said, "Nothing moves off this roadway unless I say so." Grabbing hold of his hand and removing it from my jacket, I could smell the heavy odor of alcohol on his breath. I replied, "This is a very dangerous situation. We have multiple injuries and traffic is backing up for miles. We need to clear this roadway." The chief clearly didn't like me telling him that he was not in charge, so he turned around to his crew and told them, "Help me out with this, guys." Four firefighters approached me with axes in hand, making me feel very threatened. The chief commented, "Maybe you didn't hear me the first time, but nothing moves until I say so." Before I could say another word, several of my officers stepped behind me in support. Jake Lane was one of them and holding his shotgun by his side. He asked, "Boss, do we have a problem here?" I told him, "No, but arrest anyone who refuses to put down their ax and put the chief in the back seat of my car. If he resists, cuff him." I relieved that engine company of their duties and requested a second company be dispatched. Everything from that point on was handled safely and efficiently once the second company arrived. The injured were treated, disabled vehicles were towed, the tanker was moved to a safer location, the roadway was washed of all gasoline, and the highway was cleared. By the time I returned to my car, I found the fire chief passed out in the rear seat. I was relieved to see that he wasn't in cuffs and didn't resist because the last thing I wanted to do was arrest the fire chief. I woke him up and had one of my officers take him back to his station. My shift ended at 4:00 am because of the volume of calls that later came in. By then, I was exhausted and looking forward to going home and getting some shuteye.

At 8:00 am, after catching a couple of hours of sleep, I received a phone call from the police chief's office, asking me to come in at 9:30 am. My first thought was that this was bullshit. I had worked all night and would now have to listen to some political crap about how I handled the drunken fire chief. I got dressed and stormed out of my house, ready to tell anyone and everyone what I thought and if they didn't like it, tough shit. I arrived at headquarters and was met by Captain Reynolds, who said, "Sounds like you had a busy night." Looking him straight in the eyes, I confirmed, "Yes, I did." An impish grin crossed his face and he told me that the chief wanted to see me and not to keep him waiting. Walking down the hall to his office, I kept going over in my head what I was going to say to him. When I knocked, I heard him say, "Russell, is that you banging on my door? Get in here." I entered and closed the door behind me, preparing to get my ass reamed out. Glancing up from some papers on his desk, the chief pushed his glasses down on his nose and commented, "You have been a very busy boy. Make any new friends last night?" I didn't care for the sarcasm and was about to let him know what I thought about the whole situation when he looked at me and continued, "I'm proud of you. You handled that situation just like I would have. Who the hell did they think they were screwing with?" He followed that with, "Russell, you got balls. Not many would have had the nerve to arrest a fire chief and have your men draw down on some firemen." Just to clear the point, I explained, "Chief, I didn't arrest the fire chief. I just let him sleep off a bad night." Standing up, he extended his hand to shake mine and said, "By the way, tell Lane and the rest of your crew that I said 'good job.' Now go home and get some sleep. We'll talk more about this another time and I want to hear every detail."

From that day on, my relationship with the

chief was like an uncle to a nephew. We had many long talks about a number of things, not all police-related. He passed away five years later, but was there to hand me my lieutenant's badge, which meant the world to me. I miss that man. When I think of him, I just smile. He was one of a kind.

CHAPTER 29
CANNONBALL RUN

From time to time, my junior officers became bored with the mundane day-to-day shift work, especially when working the 12:00 midnight to 8:00 am tour. They would devise games to play to keep their sanity under control during the quiet hours, which usually occurred between 3:30 and 5:30 am. I approved of none of this and they knew there would be serious consequences for their actions if they got caught. I remember one warm night in June when there was a full moon, which tends to bring out the crazy in people. My group was no exception. Just before my midnight tour began, I overheard two of the younger officers in the locker room talking about something called Cannonball Run. I knew exactly what it was because when I was younger, it was called the Breakfast Run. I asked what they knew about this and they denied knowing anything, saying only that they heard two other officers talking about it. When I asked which officers, they claimed they couldn't remember. I was proud of them for not telling on the other officers, but I knew exactly who it was. Nevertheless, there would be no Cannonball Run that night.

I suspected that Officers Joe Polk and Seth Lambert were involved. They were my squad's bad boys and were always looking for some sort of prank to pull on the rookie officers. Polk got on the job six months after me. We had gone to high school together and remained good friends. Lambert came on the job about five years later. He was several years younger than me and was politically connected. He tended to bend the rules while not breaking them, and he was a guy that would give you the shirt off his back – although it came with strings attached. I put Polk and Lambert in the same sector but in different cars so I could keep an eye on them during the night. The shift was busy up until 3:00 am, so there wasn't time for any play; it was all business. Once the shift became routinely quiet and there were very few cars on the road in their area, I knew it would be the perfect time to pull a stunt, if they were going to pull one at all.

The infamous Cannonball Run was the stunt I thought they would be planning. It was a timed race where one officer would place a personal item, such as a cover off their ticket book, a personal pad, or even one of their shoes, and place it at a designated spot on the opposite side of their sector at a mutually agreed-upon place. The other officer would leave his start area, proceed to the designated spot, pick up the personal item, and bring it back to the starting area, where the clock would then stop. Then the second officer would do the same thing as the first. Whoever had the slowest time would have to buy breakfast that morning after the shift was over.

There was only one place where it could be run safely that had very little traffic and was sparsely populated. It was a straight run, with one exception: there was a high spot on the roadway and you had to slow down while driving over it or else risk going airborne, which could cause loss of control and possible damage to the vehicle. I positioned my car on an old dirt road facing the straightaway and waited. The night was clear, the moon was full, and the sky was full of stars. With my windows down, I could hear a car coming from about a mile away. It wasn't long before I realized it was a police car because it made a very distinctive sound, almost like a rumble. I was positive it was one of my cars. Within seconds, the car flew by, but the driver had to slow down for the high spot. As soon as he reached that point, I put on my red lights and pulled him over. I was able to positively identify that it was Lambert's car. We climbed out of our cars and walked toward each other. Before I could speak, he started to say that he was chasing a speeding car, which I knew was bullshit because I had been observing that roadway for fifteen minutes and he was the only car to pass me. I asked him if that was the story he was sticking with. He realized then that he was caught doing the Cannonball Run. I directed him to get back on the road and said I would speak to him when the shift was over. That would give him a little time to sweat it out.

When the shift ended, I told Lambert to stay in the squad room because we had a few things to discuss. After lecturing him on how dangerous and irresponsible his behavior was, I explained what the consequences were. He would be assigned to Sector 1 for the next four tours. He was relieved that he wasn't getting suspended or fired and took his punishment like a man. Now, Sector 1 was a fitting punishment for this behavior. The area was the

smallest of all five sectors, covering approximately one square mile and made up of beach
bungalows, rowdy bars, and more than a fair
share of dirtbags. Since this area bordered a
beach, it required officers to get out of their car
and walk the boardwalk. It was boring as hell
and after midnight there was usually nothing
open except perhaps a few bars. There was no
variety of calls other than dealing with drunks
leaving bars and you couldn't even grab a coffee or snack because everything was closed.
Most of the cops hated working this area. It
was affectionately known as "The Barrel" because when you worked Sector 1, you were
working the bottom of the barrel.

Here comes the twist of the story. Earlier
that night, at about 2:15 am, I had checked in
at headquarters to see the lieutenant. While
there, I received a phone call from Officer
Polk, who told me all about Cannonball Run,
where it was going to take place, and at what
time. Lambert was going to go first and Polk
wanted nothing to do with it because he knew
the consequences and he had an ax to grind
with Lambert. Whatever the problem was between these two guys, this was Polk's way of
getting back at him. I thanked him for the call,
told him to go back on patrol, and said I would
handle it. To this day, Lambert has no idea that

Polk ratted him out. He just thought I was at the right place at the right time. To my knowledge, that was the night that Cannonball Run came to an end.

CHAPTER 30
NATIONAL DRAG RACES

Once a year, Jefferson Township held the Summer National Drag Races, which began on Friday afternoon and ran through Sunday evening. On this weekend, the population tripled while being visited by over one hundred thousand fans. Vendors from all over the state would come and traffic was always a disaster. The town merchants loved it because half of their income for the year was realized during that time. Our department would go on overtime mode and shift hours were doubled. The races were held at the county fairgrounds, which was approximately two hundred acres in size. The event was always held in the second week of August and temperatures would inevitably soar into the 100-degree range. This particular year was no exception, other than the fact that

the humidity was equally high, making it almost unbearable.

The tailgating parties began in the parking
lots on Friday afternoon. The parking lots were
basically large grassy areas where fans arrived
early, set up their chairs, tents, and RVs, and
then they started partying. The actual races
wouldn't begin until Saturday morning, with
the finals being held on Sunday. The meet organizers had made preparations to have tents
available for the vendors, food courts, water
stations, and first aid stations to accommodate
the anticipated crowd that would be attending. On Saturday, there was a slight chance of
showers and the temperatures held in the high
80s, with some clouds. Most people adjusted
well to the heat and the day went well, with
only a few minor incidents revolving around
excessive drinking of alcohol, disorderly con-
duct, and petty stealing from vendors.

Sunday was a completely different story. The
heat was oppressive, humidity was through
the roof, and the meet organizers miscalculat-
ed the amount of water needed for the weekend so they were running out of water. The
lines at the water stations were three deep
and fifty people long. Tempers were starting
to flare and I had to station four officers at

each of the water stations just to maintain order. The last thing I wanted to do was start arresting people because of a water shortage. Just as things were getting bad, three water trucks showed up and started selling bottled water. What bothered me most was that vendors were selling the water at triple the normal price. I headed over to one vendor and asked how he could take advantage of people who needed the water. His answer was, "Supply and demand. It's just good business." That really pissed me off and I just walked away, shaking my head. Because the heat was so brutal, I was grateful that I was working in an air-conditioned patrol car. I felt sympathy as I watched my officers on foot patrol, wearing their black uniform shirts and protective vests. I made sure that they were well hydrated by giving them cold water bottles and frequent breaks in my patrol car to cool off.

Around 3:00 pm on Sunday, I noticed a man in the lot with two small girls who I assumed were his daughters. He was in his late twenties with an athletic build and he was holding the hand of one while carrying the other in his arms. He looked exhausted and they were all sweating profusely. I motioned him to come over to my car, rolled down my window, and asked the gentleman if he and his girls were alright because they all looked like they were going to pass out. The younger girl, who the father was carrying, appeared to be about four years old. She had blonde hair and was wearing shorts and a blue top along with sandals and a visor. She innocently told me how thirsty she was and asked me if I had any water. Although I did have a bottle, I was already using it to pour onto my handkerchief so I could wipe down their faces. I asked the father why he didn't take them to the water station and he explained, "I lost my wallet about two hours ago and have been looking for it ever since. I even checked the lost and found section. I did stop at the water station but because I had no money, the vendor wouldn't sell me any, even after telling him my story. He said to come back when I had money." The father added that he came with some friends, but couldn't find them among the large crowd and didn't know how he was going to get home.

The girls looked wiped out so I seated them and the father into my air-conditioned car to cool off. After a few minutes, I drove them back to the same water station where they had been refused water and asked the vendor if he recognized the father and his two daughters. He said they had been there earlier and confirmed what the father told me. I stared him in the eye and said, "Those two little girls were on the verge of heat exhaustion and you couldn't spare some water for them? Let me tell you what's going to happen now. I'm going to take six bottles of water for my officers. Are you going to have a problem with that?" The vendor knew I was going to give some to the family, but he just answered, "Take whatever you need." I thanked him for his generosity and then left to take the family to the food court, where I bought them lunch and gave them each a bottle of cold water. When they were done, I drove them around to look for their friends but with so many people there, it was impossible to find them. I asked where they lived and the father told me they were from the next town over. I had a taxi meet us at the entrance to the fairgrounds, gave the driver a twenty-dollar bill, and instructed him to take them home. I also told the driver that if there was any additional cost, he could come back and collect the difference since I would be working there until 11:00 pm.

One week later, I received a letter that was mailed to the police department, thanking me for everything I did for the man and his two daughters. Attached was a twenty-dollar bill. The father expressed how much my kindness meant to him and how he thought I went above and beyond the call to ensure their health and safety. He also enclosed a drawing made by the two girls, showing a policeman holding the hands of two girls with great big smiles on their faces. It was one of the best gifts I have ever received. As a result of the letter, the department awarded me a commendation. During my career, I have received my fair share of awards and letters of appreciation and commendation, but this one will always be my favorite.

CHAPTER 31
THE CRAWFORDS

There was an area of town that consisted of two streets with about thirty homes. It was predominantly made up of black families. The homes were small, with a bungalow or cottage-like appearance, and most needed some TLC or cosmetic enhancements. On the upside, the properties were well-maintained with respect to yard maintenance and we rarely had any major complaints from the residents. In fact, many of them were distantly related to each other and their families had occupied the land for generations. Every once in a while, there would be a call about a family dispute or a minor problem with a neighbor.

On one particular Friday night, there was a call for assistance to mediate a family problem. The sector car responded and cleared the call a few minutes later. Shortly after leaving, a second and then a third call came in from the same address, stating that assistance was still needed. The officer was getting tired of responding to the situation, involving an elderly couple that been quarreling all night, and he was frustrated that they weren't listening. After the third call came in, I met with the sector car and asked Officer Rossi what the problem was. He advised me that the couple was having marital problems and the way they were drinking too much alcohol wasn't helping the situation; it was only escalating it.

I had been monitoring the amount of calls that the area car had been dispatched to and I recognized the address. It was the Crawford house. These people were in their eighties and had been married for more than sixty years. I knew them well. I advised headquarters that if there should be a return call to that address, I would be the one to respond and handle the dispute. It wasn't long before the fourth call came in. I advised dispatch that I was responding and there would be no need for a sector car to show up at the Crawford address. This couple was the sweetest and nicest you would ever want to meet. Whenever I drove down their street in the past, they always seemed to be holding hands or gardening together. They often waved at me as I passed their home and even invited me in on occasion for some homemade lemonade.

I walked toward their house and could see Mr. Crawford sitting in his favorite rocking chair on the front porch with a large jug of what appeared to be homemade booze. He was a small man with a slight build and short gray hair. He always wore a hat and his face always looked like he hadn't shaved in days. Anytime I had ever seen him, he was wearing the same clothes: a plaid shirt, faded black pants, suspenders and a belt, socks, and a beat-up pair of shoes. But he had a perpetual smile and I often complimented him on his front gold tooth, which you could see when he smiled. He was a happy-go-lucky fellow and had a charismatic personality. Everyone loved him. As I approached the porch, Mr. Crawford looked up at me and said, "Sergeant Dennis, what are you doing here?" I responded, "This is not a social call. What's going on with you and Mrs. Crawford?" Shaking his head from side to side, he replied, "It's the wife. She be getting crazy in her old age. She came at me with a broom for no reason at all." After a lengthy conversation with him, I was able to determine that Mrs. Coleman, the widow who lived next door, had made a pass at Mr. Crawford. His wife found out and thought it was disgraceful. He, on the other hand, was flattered by being hit on by this younger neighbor in her seventies and seemed to be enjoying it.

Now, Mrs. Crawford was in her eighties. She was a tiny woman, standing at about 4'6" at best, and hunched over when she walked. She had white hair that was always pulled back into a bun and wore a long kitchen apron over her clothing. She proudly wore her wedding band and a set of rosary beads that hung around her neck as a necklace. She took pride in her physical appearance, yet her attempts at putting on makeup left a lot to be desired since her lipstick covered more than her mouth and she wore too much blue eye shadow. She always smelled of Mr. Crawford's Old Spice cologne. The three things she loved most were her God, her bible, and her husband. She was the friendliest and kindest woman and always wanted to give me a kiss on the cheek.

Mrs. Crawford saw me on the porch talking to her husband and came outside carrying her broom, which she attempted to swat her husband with. Seeing him holding his jug and her clutching her broom was truly a sight. I had to summon all of my inner strength not to burst out laughing at this sweet little old couple. I felt like I was refereeing the munchkins. She told me she wanted a divorce because she felt disrespected that he was enjoying the neighbor coming on to him. I advised her that she couldn't keep hitting him with the broom and that it wouldn't solve anything. In fact, the more she hit him, the more he drank. I also informed her that we couldn't keep coming back because it was taking resources away from the rest of the area and if it continued, they would leave the police no choice but to arrest one or both of them.

Neither of them wanted the other to be arrested, but I couldn't leave them this way or we would certainly be coming back. I started thinking creatively and outside the box. Glancing at them and biting my lip, I devised a plan that just might solve the problem. At this point, they were both adamant about wanting a divorce, so I asked Mrs. Crawford, "Do you still want that divorce you were asking for?" She held up the broom, shook it at her husband, and said, "You bet I does." Turning toward Mr. Crawford, I asked him the same question. He replied, "Give the crazy old bitch what she wants. There are plenty of other women who want me. I'm a catch." Putting my hand over my mouth to keep from smiling, I stated, "Both of you come here and place your right hand on my chest over my badge." After they did, I continued, "By the power given to me by the governor and the Lord thy God, I hereby now divorce you both." Mrs. Crawford smiled and looked at Mr. Crawford. She told him now that he was single, he couldn't share her bed and that he should sleep on the couch. Mr. Crawford acknowledged her, then looked at me and told me there would be no more problems tonight. They thanked me and Mrs. Crawford gave me a kiss on the cheek. I left their house at about 9:00 pm, hoping that would be the last of them, and finished out the rest of my shift without any further calls to their place.

I pulled into headquarters at about 7:45 am after working a double shift. I was exhausted and looking forward to going home and getting some sleep when headquarters received a call from the Crawford residence, requesting that I return. Turning my car around, I proceeded back to their home. When I pulled up in front, I found the Crawfords holding hands. I approached them and before I could speak, Mrs. Crawford told me, "We changed our minds. Could you undo our divorce?" They were both smiling and obviously regretted their actions of the night before. I asked them if they were sure that they wanted me to do this. When they both nodded, I instructed them to each put their right hand on my chest over my badge. Going through the same procedure, I stated, "By the power given to me by the governor and the Lord thy God, I hereby undo your divorce and declare you married again." Within seconds, they were hugging and kissing each other and thanking me again. Mrs. Crawford leaned over to give me my usual kiss on the cheek and invited me to stay for breakfast. I graciously declined and told her I would take a rain check. She smiled and went into the house as Mr. Crawford walked me to my car. He tapped me on the shoulder, leaned in, and whispered, "Just so you know, I am one hell of a catch." I drove away and laughed all the way back to headquarters.

CHAPTER 32
PROMOTION TO LIEUTENANT

Another milestone was happening. I had been on the job for almost twenty years and was being promoted to the rank of lieutenant. It was difficult to believe how the time went by so quickly. Sitting on a chair in my living room, I found myself drifting back, recalling both the good and the bad experiences that had brought me to this moment in time. One thought was that I would be leaving my officers because when a sergeant got promoted to a lieutenant or watch commander, the policy of the department was to keep you in the building doing administrative work. Instead of being a squad sergeant where your responsibilities were looking over six to eight men, you were now in charge of three squads that included twenty to thirty officers. I knew that as a lieutenant, I would have to micromanage and be responsible for ensuring that my sub-ordinate officers, sergeants included, followed all rules and regulations. It would also include the issuance of directives to subordinates about new and revised policies, preparing staff reports, and assisting in performance evalua-tions of my subordinates.

My squad was like a family because I some-times felt I spent more time with them than my own family. Telling them would be ex-tremely sad and difficult. I knew they would be happy for me and wanted me to succeed, but it was going to be a major adjustment in my life. Just thinking about the responsibili-ties of a shift commander was overwhelming. My ultimate goal was to be the chief of the department and to get there, I knew I would have to pay my dues. As I stood in front of the mirror, looking back at me was a man in his full dress uniform, with dress white shirt, formal navy blue uniform pants, and formal navy blue jacket with gold buttons down the front. The jacket was also adorned with all of my award bars on the left side on my chest.

I was nervous, but confident that this next step up the ladder was going to be a positive one. It was two hours until the big moment when I heard the phone ring. The voice on the other end of the call brought a huge smile to my face. It was the chief. In that gravelly, rough voice that I dreaded hearing on so many occasions, he said, "This is your night. Are you ready?" Hearing his voice calmed me down and I replied, "Absolutely." He responded, "I'm proud of you. You'll make a great commander. I have one request. May I present you with your badge?" I assured him I wouldn't want it any other way. His voice trailed off and he told me that he would see me later.

As great a night it was going to be for me personally, there were others being promoted to lieutenant, as well. These were men that I came up the ranks with, including C.J. Steiner, Pudge Di Silva, Sal Alfano, Ted Roland, and Don Fisher. They were all standup guys and deserving of their promotions. The ceremony began and one by one, the new lieutenants were sworn in. I remember when my name was called. I had been sitting in the reserved row, then stood up and walked across the floor to approach the chief. I stopped directly in front of him and gave him a hand salute. He returned the salute as the town clerk stepped in and asked me to place my hand on the bible, which my father came up to hold. As the clerk read the official words, I looked into my father's eyes and could see a few tears of pride and joy running down his face. Of course, that led to a tear or two welling up in my own eyes. It gave me tremendous joy to see the pride on my father's face. The mayor came over and congratulated me after handing me my lieutenant bars and my father then gave me a big hug and a kiss on the cheek. As I turned, the chief extended his hand to shake mine and, with a huge smile, presented me with my new badge and passed off his old lieutenant bars to me. He commented, "I hope these bring you as much luck as they did me." I assured him, "I consider it an honor to wear your bars."

As the ceremony concluded, I was told to report to Captain Reynold's office that Monday morning for my new assignment and was given the weekend off. The next phase of my career was about to begin.

CHAPTER 33
A HOSTAGE NEGOTIATION

My first shift assignment as a lieutenant lasted less than a year. The previous chief had retired within that first year due to illness and a position was made for a new chief. Stepping into that role was Chief LaRocca, a medium-sized guy about 5'9" tall with salt and pepper hair. He was distinctly Italian and walked with a swagger. He was quite familiar with me because we had worked together on many occasions when I was assigned to the Narcotics Unit. He was very political and there was no doubt in my mind that the mayor promoted him to the chief's position because their thinking was on the same page. He was nothing like the old chief and his work ethic was more like that of a politician than of a chief. Consequently, we banged heads on many issues, yet he respected and valued my opinions.

We had coffee together most mornings and he usually bounced ideas and decisions off me. I recommended those that were more in tune with the way a police department should run, yet he still made politically-based decisions on the hiring of new officers, assignments, and budgeting, most of which revolved around friendships and politics. After prolonged discussions, he decided I should be assigned to his personal staff.

One of the many assignments I was given was heading up the Internal Affairs Division. This was not a position I wanted because it meant I would be investigating complaints registered against other officers, reporting my findings, and making recommended charges to the chief. When I was not conducting investigations against officers, to keep me out of his hair he would send me to school for classes in arson investigation, sex crimes, and homicides so I could come back and teach those fundamentals to our supervisors. He later sent me to school for a two-week course to become our department's hostage negotiator. It seemed that all I did was attend school and teach classes and as a result, I felt I was moving further and further away from performing police work. I missed working the streets and being out in the field. Little did I know how quickly my hostage negotiating training would be used and how much it would help me in a multitude of situations.

Almost three months after my negotiator training was completed, I was asked to negotiate the release of a two-year-old child who was being held at knifepoint by his father. The father was denied visitation rights by the court because they felt he was unfit due to a drug conviction from years earlier. The father's attitude was, "If I can't have my son, then no one will." The patrols were initially sent to the apartment because of a domestic dispute between a couple. When they arrived, they found the man and woman fighting over the court's ruling pertaining to their child. At one point, the father went into the bedroom, picked up the child, and was going to leave. When confronted by the officers, he pulled a knife out of his pocket and placed it to the throat of the child, threatening to kill him. When their attempts to resolve the situation failed, I was called.

When I arrived at the scene, I was met by Big Joe Morris, who had recently been promoted to sergeant. He advised me of the problem his officers were having with the irate father and that a knife was at the throat of a small child. Upon entering the apartment, I noticed how hot it was. There was no air conditioning on and I could see that the father and son were covered in sweat. The child was crying and the mother informed us that he hadn't been fed in hours. The foul odor coming from the baby's diaper indicated that he needed to be changed. The man was continuing to yell at the officers and made it perfectly clear what would happen if his demands weren't met. I asked the officers to step back and let me try to calmly speak to the man to see if we could meet some of his demands. I tried to impress upon him that my main concern was for the welfare of the child and in no way did I want any harm to come to the child or him.

He explained to me that when he was eighteen and hanging out with the wrong crowd, he was arrested for drug possession, namely marijuana. It was now twenty years later and he was the father of a two-year-old boy and divorced from his child's mother. He had gotten his life together and had a good job as a foreman in the local factory. He had always gotten along with his ex-wife and would often come by to visit his son without incident. Apparently, his ex-wife was now engaged to be married and her fiancé resented the father's visits with the mother and child and basically wanted him out of the picture. As a result, he convinced his future wife to petition the court to have the father's visitation rights revoked. There was an order handed down by the court, pending an investigation to revoke his visitation rights based on his earlier drug charge from many years ago. There had been three months of no visitation and he was frustrated with the way the court system was handling the investigation and not being able to see his son, so he decided to take matters into his own hands. This was when the altercation started.

Our conversation dragged on for nearly two hours as he told me his story and that all he wanted was to be a part of his son's life. The child was still crying and beginning to show signs of dehydration, so I suggested we get some fluids in his son, change the baby's diaper and clothes, and possibly give him some food. I reminded the man that this was his son and if he truly loved him as much as he claimed, then he should address his baby's needs. I could see that he was starting to weaken and the knife wasn't pressed as tightly against the child's throat as it was earlier. I knew by looking at him that he didn't want to hurt his son. He wasn't thinking clearly. He just wanted to be listened to and to make a statement on how unfair the whole situation was, because he was never given the opportunity to speak before his visitation was revoked.

I noticed a diaper bag on the floor next to the table where we sat and asked if he could reach for the bag so we could change the child's diaper. He would have to put down the knife in order to do that and I knew I could then make my move. When he lowered the knife to reach for the bag, I quickly grabbed the child. Two officers, who had been listening to our conversation, moved toward the table and jumped on the father. As the knife fell to the floor, he was handcuffed and placed under arrest and the child was turned over to the first aid squad. The child had a slight cut on his throat and I wanted him taken to the hospital and thoroughly checked by a doctor to be sure he was fine. The total time of the incident, from the initial call to the arrest, was about six hours. The safe outcome of the child was definitely worth the time, but it was certainly the longest six hours of my life.

The true tragedy in this incident was the fact that this was a man who had made a mistake twenty years earlier, turned his life around, and became a productive citizen but because of a flawed system, he was being denied his right to see his own son. As a result of his frustration with the court system and taking matters into his own hands, he once again crossed the line and became a member of criminal society.

CHAPTER 34
INTERNAL AFFAIRS

As stated earlier, within my first year of serving as a lieutenant, I was put in charge of the Internal Affairs division under new Police Chief LaRocca. I was uncomfortable with this new assignment because I would be investigating incidents and suspicions of unlawful and professional misconduct attributed to officers in my police department. I found it unimaginable that officers who were sworn to protect and serve would degrade their oath of office and be part of the criminal element. However, I also realized that there were officers who took advantage of their position. My thought was, "With absolute power comes absolute responsibility."

When investigating a complaint, it was difficult for me not to be biased, but I had to constantly remind myself that each officer was a reflection of the department. If there was any legitimacy to the complaint, it was my obligation, based on my findings, to recommend disciplinary action or termination to the chief and then he would decide. I rarely recommended termination, but when I did, it was because the evidence of serious wrongdoing was overwhelming.

One such investigation dealt with excessive force and it wasn't prompted by only one particular incident; it was based on several different complaints from several victims. The chief called me into his office one day and explained that there were some serious allegations leveled against Officer Kyle Peterson. He had two years on the job and had been through three different training officers. After his initial one-year probationary period ended, his training officer recommended that it be extended for an additional six months due to Peterson's demonstration of lack of patience with the public. The chief agreed and Peterson was given a different training officer. After another six months, his new training officer recommended yet another extended probationary period due to the same problems. Peterson was now constantly questioning his authority and when anyone questioned him, he became aggressive. This usually ended with him making an arrest and adding an additional charge of resisting arrest. This pattern was becoming the norm, which is why it eventually went to Internal Affairs.

The chief gave me Peterson's personnel file, which dated all the way back from his academy days until the present. Reading it, I found it very difficult to comprehend how he was ever hired in the first place. First and foremost, he scored very low on the psychological profile. In addition, there were many incident reports from instructors and training officers, all indicating that they had concerns that his aggressive tendencies and his inability to control his temper would eventually become problematic to the department. Why their recommendations weren't heeded was a puzzlement to me.

After a three-week investigation and numerous interviews with the complainants, it was determined that the common factors in all of these complaints were over-aggressiveness, lack of patience, and perceived attacks on Peterson's authority as a police officer. I also found that each of Officer Peterson's reports included arrests accompanied with resisting and assaults on him. For these reasons, I finally concluded that an additional extension of his probation would not be the answer. The problems were ongoing, so in the best interest of the department, I recommended termination of the officer. My entire report was given to the chief. After reading it, he asked if I had personally spoken with the officer and I confirmed that I had. He inquired about the officer's demeanor during my interview with him. I told the chief that Peterson was confrontational, highly excited, and overly aggressive, at one point picking up my coffee mug and slamming it on my desk. I also relayed that I had told the officer he was being insubordinate, our conversation was over, and had asked him to leave. As Peterson was exiting my office, he stopped, turned around, pointed his finger at me, and warned, "This is not over by a long shot. Councilman Gallagher will hear about this." Ultimately, I informed the chief that I was standing by my report and recommendation.

A few days later, Officer Peterson was called in for a meeting with Chief LaRocca and Captain Reynolds, where he was advised of the findings and recommendation. When the chief informed him of his termination, he became violent, throwing chairs and papers and threatening his two superiors. The chief ultimately had to call additional officers into his office to restrain Peterson. His weapon and badge were taken and he was escorted out of the building.

Because I was off the day that meeting took place, the chief called me later to inform me about his decision to terminate and the incident that had taken place in his office. He was extremely upset that someone with such a violent and aggressive nature could have slipped through the cracks. Without wanting to appear condescending, I told him that all the signs were there and that someone obviously chose not to listen. This particular officer was hired prior to LaRocca becoming the chief, but now that he was in charge of the department, he was ultimately responsible for each and every officer. I suggested that he actually read Peterson's file, especially the pages that included the recommendation letters written by people who endorsed him for the job. Out of the six names listed, five were politically involved with running our town – including Councilman Gallagher, who just happened to be Peterson's uncle. I told the chief, "He didn't fall through the cracks. He was escorted through the front door by politicians and we were left to deal with the mess that was made." I thought my career was going to end as a lieutenant because of my outspokenness, but I was lucky. I always respected the position of the chief and he knew that. I'm sure certain political factions were not happy with my evaluations and recommendations, but as the years went on and our politicians changed, this would eventually change, also.

CHAPTER 35
MY TIME WITH THE CHIEF

As the years passed, I handled many more investigations but only a few more hostage situations. The chief expanded my investigative staff and I now had two additional sergeants. I was beginning to catch the eyes of certain political newcomers. The "Old Guard" was changing and a new and more progressive department was rising from the ashes. I was summoned to an executive staff meeting in the chief's office. All division heads were there and the topic of discussion was the replacement of retiring captains. There were five division heads, four of which would be retiring within the next three months. Two were at mandatory age and two had health problems. It was at this point that the chief informed me that he was going to promote me to the rank of captain and the recommendation of all division heads was that I take over the Detective Division. I'm sure my years of conducting investigations were a determining factor.

Chief LaRocca was still very loyal to the Old Guard, but their political influence was dwindling. During a strictly off-the-record conversation with LaRocca, I was told he needed me to act as a buffer between him and the new politicians. This was unfamiliar territory for me, mainly because I had never engaged in politics but at this new level, I could see where it might become necessary. Budgets, manpower, and equipment were all used as tools to manipulate leverage to achieve certain gains. This was a game I would have to learn quickly to survive.

Captain Bill McCoy was the retiring detective division commander and it was at his personal request that I take over his division. In the weeks prior to his leaving, we had many sit-downs that were a great help to me. I can recall one day meeting with him to review every detective's personnel file and getting his perspective on the strengths and weaknesses of each. I will always remember him saying that day, "I couldn't have gotten a better replacement. I've watched you from the beginning. You were made for this. I wish you all the luck and don't forget to visit me when I retire." Bill's health wasn't good, and unfortunately he didn't get to enjoy his retirement for too long. One year later, he passed away on Christmas Day. I was so saddened by his death that I made a promise to myself to continue his legacy of excellence as a division commander and captain.

I was beginning to settle in as captain and the commander of the Detective Division. Just the sound of that title was a little unsettling because it conjured up all kinds of responsibilities. I could recall being responsible as a sergeant for just my squad of eight men and now my responsibilities encompassed the departments of Criminal, Juvenile, Evidence, Forensics, Psychological Counseling, DARE (Drug Alcohol Resistance Education), and in-school resource officers, not to mention civilian personnel. The police department was changing and I was about to play a major role in that development.

There were five captains and seniority-wise, I was the junior captain. However, the chief heavily relied on my opinions and trusted me to speak for him in his absence. Whenever anything controversial came up, he always called and asked me to handle it. The chief was spending less time in the office and more time at private meetings. I learned that those private meetings were with different politicians, where the decisions being made were not always in the best interest of the department.

I also encountered some personnel problems. Chief LaRocca had his favorites, but there were also officers he despised. Although I was one of his favorites, he would dump officers who he didn't care for in my division and ask me to straighten them out. I was angry because they didn't want to be there and pushing them to work productively was a strain on my manpower. The only way I could get them to become better detectives was to send them to school, but for the detectives that the chief disliked, this solution was out of the question. Therein was my dilemma. How could I help them to become more productive when I couldn't provide the necessary tools to make that happen? I decided that if I couldn't go through the front door, then I would go through the back window. I had to change tactics. The chief wouldn't send them to school because he saw that as a benefit, so I needed to devise a plan that would make him believe that they wouldn't go to any school under any circumstances, because they liked sitting around doing nothing.

I was getting ready to leave for the day when I was summoned to the chief's office. He was in a foul mood and ranting about one particular officer named Arthur Chapel. He was number one on the chief's shit list. Chapel was a good officer, but he was a loner. He didn't work well with others, but if I gave him a case to work on by himself, he was a pit bull. He did anything I asked of him without complaining and he did it well. My one problem was that the chief refused to let him attend any school, yet I needed Chapel to become better versed in certain new and changing laws and procedures. The next day, I stormed into the chief's office, sat in my chair, and did my best to look pissed off. Of course, his first words were, "What's up with you?" I complained, "You saddled me with Chapel and all he does is sit at his desk and read the newspaper. He laughs at the other detectives and tells them what chumps they are for working so hard while he gets paid to do nothing." I then told the chief that Chapel said he wouldn't attend any school we might send him to and that he had it made right where he was. The chief's eyes got big, his face became flushed, and he stared into space before finally responding, "Oh, really? Well, you can tell that lazy bum that I said his goofing around days are over and he will go to any school you see fit.

Do I make myself clear?" Looking seriously at the chief, I replied, "He's not going to like that at all." The chief's answer was, "Tough shit." I sighed, "Alright, you're the boss" and left, managing to hide the smile on my face.

Of course, Chapel had never said any of what I relayed to the chief. In fact, he asked me every day if he could attend classes to get more training, but the chief would always turn it down. He had a thirst for knowledge but it was never going to happen because the chief didn't like him. As I exited the chief's office, I realized that my plan, as devious and simple as it was, was now in motion. All of my detectives would be getting the training they needed to become productive. This would become the first of many times that I played this game with the chief.

Ironically, by the time Chapel left my command, he had attended more than fourteen schools and became one of my best detectives. He solved high-profile crimes and received numerous awards and citations for excellence, which ultimately made the chief look good.

Although some officers had difficulty obtaining Chief LaRocca's approval to attend school, I was not one of them. In fact, the chief used to send me to every one of them, whether I wanted it or not. There I was, a captain in charge of a division, constantly going to classes – most of which I could teach. Sometimes I think it was just to get me out of his sight. He liked me very much and respected my opinion, but we didn't always agree on controversial issues and I wasn't politically motivated. I often told him that he should be sending the sergeants and possibly a lieutenant to schools so they could teach the men working for them, but it fell on deaf ears.

I finally decided that I had had enough. There had to be a way to end this nonsense. The wheels in my head started spinning until a plan was formulated. I received a notice advising me to report to yet another school. This particular class was one that I had taught at the police academy years earlier. Rather than complain, I attended the two-week-long class on Tactical Approaches to Crimes in Progress. It was an easy two weeks and it felt like I was on vacation. When I reported back to the chief a few weeks later, I would have a surprise for him. A week into the class, I contacted a personal friend who owned and operated an embroidery company and asked her for a favor. I inquired if she could make up two collared golf shirts with a specific special logo. She assured me it would be no problem. The next thing I did was give her the logo design and the wording to be used. A week later, I picked up my shirts and they were perfect. I was ecstatic with the final product.

The class was now over, I had the weekend off, and I found myself constantly grinning to myself because I knew my plan was going to work. That Monday morning, I went into work carrying my briefcase and wearing my departmental blazer, which covered my customized shirt. I headed directly to my office and was advised by my secretary that the chief wanted to see me as soon as I came in. Giggling to myself, I took off my blazer and hung it up, picked up my coffee cup, and went across the hall to see the chief. He was writing some letters with his head down as I entered, and without looking up, he asked, "How was school?" I responded, "It was good. I brought you back a gift from the class." I then placed his new, neatly folded shirt on top of his desk. Glancing at the shirt and seeing the logo, he then looked up directly at me. I was wearing the exact same shirt. He rose from his chair, adjusted his glasses to make sure he was seeing clearly, and exclaimed, "Holy Christ! What the hell is this? I can't wear this shirt and you can't wear that, either." I asked him why in disbelief. His words became incoherent while I tried not to bite my lip and asked him what the problem was. It seemed he was offended by the shirt's logo. It was a nicely embroidered golf shirt with two crossed pistols in gold on the left side and the letters "S.H.I.T." underneath in one-inch letters. He asked me what the hell kind of a school this was, to which I told him, "Special Handling of Innovative Tactics." He stood there staring and shaking his head before relenting, "Alright, you win. No more schools for you." Returning to my office, I thought with satisfaction, "Bazingga."

The chief was now within a year of his mandatory retirement age and each day his mood swings were becoming more apparent. On any given day, anything could set him off. I recall one particular day when he was reading a memo sent to us by the F.B.I. that dealt with terrorism and how we should never let our guard down. While attending staff meetings or sitting in our offices, all five of us captains routinely had a bad habit of taking off our weapons and securing them in our desk drawers. If the chief ever called me into his office for any reason, I would always put my weapon back on. The crazy part was that he never wore his own weapon. If, on occasion, I forgot to put mine on or if I accidentally ran into him in the hallway without it, he would give me a lengthy lecture about protocol pertaining to terroristic attacks in public buildings. I found it hard to fathom that terrorists could enter our police complex, bypass a state-of-the-art security system, and get past at least forty officers without hearing some sort of commotion. Nevertheless, he wanted all division commanders wearing their weapons. One day, my secretary and the chief's secretary were having coffee in the break room. His secretary was complaining that the chief was in one of his moods and was going to call a surprise staff meeting. In anticipation of his assumption that the division commanders would not be wearing their duty weapons, he had her write five letters of reprimand, one for each of us. There would be no substance to the meeting so when we showed, he would ask to see our guns and if we weren't wearing them, he would personally hand out the written reprimands. My secretary relayed this information to me. The chief was going to make an example of all his staff, except one, and that would be me.

At 11:00 am, the call from the chief's office came in, directing the five captains to report to his office immediately for a special meeting. One by one, all the commanders showed up, taking their usual seats until everyone arrived. Chief LaRocca, looking stern and carrying a handful of letters, examined all of us and with his raised tone of voice, said, "I'm sick and tired of you all not paying attention to my directives and those of the F.B.I. on terrorism and awareness." He then called on each of us individually to physically show him our duty weapon. One by one, he handed out a lecture and letter of reprimand to the four other captains who were not wearing their weapons. I was the last one, so when he got to me, he asked me to show him my weapon as he was already holding up and shaking the reprimand that was meant for me. He demanded, "Take it. You're the biggest violator of the bunch." Smiling back at him, I opened my blazer and pulled back the right side, exposing my beautiful 40 caliber Beretta in its holster. I replied, "You mean this weapon? I was just telling the other commanders about the terrorism memo when you called. I think you can hold onto that letter. I don't think I'll be needing it today." The expression on his face was priceless. He was beet red, his lips were mumbling, and you could see that I had gotten the best of him. He crumpled up the letter in his hand and threw it at me, warning, "One of these days, there will come a day." Smiling again, I agreed, "You're probably right, but not today." With that, he yelled and told us to leave his office.

I caught all kinds of grief from the others for days. They knew I was the biggest violator but couldn't figure out how I knew to wear my gun that day. To be honest, I was quite surprised that Captain C.J. Steiner, who was in charge of the Patrol Division, wasn't wearing his weapon. He notoriously carried his duty gun, a small belly gun, and one in his ankle holster. He just happened to be in the armory that morning cleaning all of his weapons, so when the call came in, he just left right away. There would be many more surprise meetings with the chief, but we would never be caught unprepared.

CHAPTER 36
MY DAUGHTER

One of the biggest joys in my life was having my children. I always prided myself on teaching them the fundamentals of being a good person. I encouraged them to share and to stand against racism and bullying and I taught them to always stick up for others, especially if they couldn't stick up for themselves. I never realized that these lessons would once again require my presence in the principal's office with my six-year-old daughter.

Because my wife and I both worked, my parents – namely my mother, who lived nearby – volunteered to pick up my daughter every day after school and take care of her until we got home. She was blessed to have the opportunity to spend quality time with her grandparents. During this time, she was becoming extremely influenced, especially by my mother, who was born and raised in New York City. I recall growing up in the city in the early 1950s and being taken care of by numerous relatives and neighbors. This affected speech patterns, reflection on ethnic groups, and the use of words to describe different things or people. For example, everyone was known by their first name and their ethnic background. For instance, my Irish friend was known as Danny the Mick or my Italian friend was Tony the Guinea. No one took it as disrespectful because the neighborhood was a melting pot of people, made up of different nationalities and ethnicities.

I was now a newly promoted captain and taking my responsibilities as a division commander seriously. This involved overseeing the Detective Bureau, which was broken down into Juvenile and Criminal, plus the D.A.R.E. (Drug Abuse Resistance Education) Program, which sent an officer into the schools and taught the elementary school students about the dangers of drugs, alcohol, and bullying. The program was tailored to the specific ages of students in each grade. On many occasions, I would accompany the D.A.R.E. officer and talk with the students, as well as the parents, in hopes of promoting a positive image for all police officers.

There was one occasion when my D.A.R.E. officer was going to be in my daughter's school and the topic of his discussion was going to be about the students' parents and how they could be a positive influence. He always started his lecture by asking each child what their parents did for a living. He told me that when he got to my daughter, Jessica, he planned to make a big fuss when she told the class that her daddy was not only a police officer, but Chief of Detectives. I told him that was a great idea and to let me know how he made out.

On the day he attended my daughter's school, I received a call from her principal, requesting my presence. It took me by surprise because I hadn't been summoned to a school in eight years, since my son Michael's escapades. I didn't have a clue as to why I was being called down because my daughter Jessica was such a sweet little girl, worked hard in class, and never had any behavior issues. My first concern was that she was hurt or sick, so I rushed over to her school and was directed to the principal's office. As I hurried down the hall, I could see Jessica sitting on a bench, coloring in her new D.A.R.E coloring book with crayons. Her feet were dangling because they couldn't reach the floor and she was smiling. As soon as she saw me, her face lit up and she yelled out, "Daddy!" and jumped into my arms, excited to see me. I was immediately relieved, knowing that she was fine. She didn't seem to have a clue as to why I was there and sat back down to continue her coloring as I went into the office. I was led into a private room with Mrs. Brady, the principal, along with her teacher, Ms. Fowler, and Officer Soloman from my D.A.R.E. program. Mrs. Brady thanked me for coming so quickly and asked me to take a seat. She then asked with concern, "Do we have a problem at home?" I was essentially dumbfounded by that question and didn't know what she was talking about, not to mention why Officer Soloman would be present at a meeting regarding my child. Seeing the confusion on my face, Mrs. Brady said she thought my D.A.R.E. officer could explain it better than she could.

Turning to Officer Soloman, who appeared uncomfortable, I asked, "Well? What's going on?" That's when he explained that he had visited Jessica's class earlier that day and asked each of the kids what their parents did for a living. He and I had discussed this earlier that morning but I still couldn't figure out where this was going. Then he dropped the bomb on me. Apparently, after asking each student about their parents and hearing that they were teachers, secretaries, or doctors, he got to Jessica and asked her what her daddy did. He was expecting her to say that I was a police officer, but instead she blurted out with pride that her daddy was an alcoholic. Officer Soloman was so shaken at her response that he quickly moved on to the next child while Ms. Fowler stood in the classroom, horrified. I was speechless at first and couldn't imagine why my daughter would say this, since I wasn't a drinker. I asked if we could bring her in to discuss the issue. Mrs. Fowler brought in Jessica, who sat on my lap. I asked her if she remembered Officer Soloman and what his job was and she confirmed that she knew him and that he was the D.A.R.E. officer who gave her a coloring book. I then asked her what she told the class about what my job was. She excitedly said, "Yes! I told my class that you were an alcoholic." There was dead silence in the room and all eyes were now on me. After I composed myself, I looked directly into her hazel eyes and asked if she knew what an alcoholic was. Her answer was equally dumbfounding. She said no, but that she heard that word on television at her grandmother's house and thought it sounded really important. I asked her if she didn't she think that being a police officer and Chief of Detectives was important. She said yes, but the other word sounded better. When I explained to her what an alcoholic was, she told everyone in the room that I only drank iced tea.

Once my daughter cleared up the confusion, the demeanor of the group became lighter and everyone began to laugh. Mrs. Brady told Jessica what a beautiful little girl she was and how proud she was for clearing up the misunderstanding. She then motioned for her to come to her desk, opened the drawer, and told her she could have a lollipop. Jessica, being Jessica, reached in and instead of grabbing just one, grabbed five lollipops. The principal merely smiled and laughed that it was fine. I thanked the women for being so concerned about my daughter's welfare and thanked Officer Soloman for giving the children a presentation. As I left the office holding Jessica's hand, I asked her why she took five lollipops instead of one. She told me she had four other friends that she wanted to share them with. At that moment, I felt proud of my daughter, knowing she was practicing one of the virtues I instilled in her about not being selfish.

It never ceased to amaze me how my daughter continued to demonstrate how to be a good friend to others. There was an occasion where she had been at school and was having lunch with her friend, Leon Chin, when a group of students her age came over and began taunting Leon. Jessica, having been taught that bullying was unacceptable in any form, stood up and defended him. Words were exchanged and the group walked away. However, I still received a call from the principal requesting my presence in her office. When I arrived, it seemed like deja vu because my daughter was sitting on the bench right outside the office, looking sweet and angelic and rocking her legs back and forth. As usual, when she saw me, there was excitement and a great big smile on her face. When asked why I was there again, she couldn't tell me because she was unsure. Inside, Mrs. Brady told me that it had come to her attention that there was an incident in the lunchroom involving Jessica that needed an explanation. Jessica was apparently being accused of being a racist, which I found extremely hard to believe because my wife and I had always taught her to accept other people's cultural and ethnic differences. I felt it necessary to bring Jessica in to explain what had transpired during lunch. She said, "Dad, you've always taught me to stand up for people who were being bullied and made fun of and I did." I was extremely proud that she was practicing the ideals that I had instilled in her. Annoyed, I turned toward Mrs. Brady and before I could say a word, she said, "Jessica, tell Daddy the whole story." Jessica continued, "Well, Dad, we were having lunch when the two Polaks and the black girl started teasing Leon, the Chink, so I had to stick up for him like you told me to." Hearing those words, I wanted to crawl under a desk. Mrs. Brady told me she knew there must be an explanation for this, so she asked Jessica why she used those ethnic words. My daughter appeared stunned and then explained that whenever her Nana (my mother) picked her up at school, Jessica would point out her friends and Nana referred to them as the Polaks, the blacks, and the Chinks. I was never so embarrassed because my daughter never knew what racism was. She was only repeating what her grandmother said. I humbly apologized for my daughter's actions, assured Mrs. Brady that this behavior would be corrected, and then left the school. Once home, I called my mother and explained what happened at school and told her that she couldn't speak that way in front of Jessica or I would make alternate arrangements to have her picked up from school.

My mother spent fifty years living in New York City in a multicultural neighborhood, where people were identified by their ethnic background and didn't take offense to it.

Although she meant no disrespect, I advised her that these types of references were unacceptable and would not be tolerated when spoken in front of my children. After my talk with Jessica and her Nana, there were no more calls at work to report to the principal's office.

CHAPTER 37
GASOLINE MAN

There was another negotiation many years later, involving a man threatening to commit suicide if his demands weren't met. It was on a cool Friday night in September and I was enjoying the night with my twelve-year old-daughter. My second marriage had failed, so I only got to see my daughter every other weekend. We had gone out to dinner earlier and then watched some television before I put her to bed. I had a one-bedroom apartment, so she would sleep on the sofa bed in the living room while I slept in the bedroom. I remember my beeper going off at about 1:00 am, indicating that I should call headquarters. I recognized the number as that of the shift commander. Checking my list of commanders to see who was working, I realized it was Lieutenant Pudge DiSilva, who was a bit of an alarmist. I didn't have a clue as to why he was beeping me, but within seconds another page came in, only this time 911 was attached. The standard operating procedure for the use of 911 meant that there was an emergency and to respond at once.

I immediately responded and called him back. Pudge was on the verge of a nervous breakdown. Once I calmed him down enough to find out what was happening, he informed me that there was a crazy man in the apartment complex directly behind headquarters who had poured gallons of gasoline all over himself and his apartment. He was threatening to set the complex on fire. I told him to notify the chief, have the fire company from that district stand by, and direct the police officers to start evacuating the residents in the surrounding area. I also instructed him to log me on duty and that I would be responding to the scene. I only lived a few minutes away, but I could not leave my daughter alone in the apartment, so I called my girlfriend Kathleen, who lived directly across the street, and had her come to my place and sleep in my bed. If my daughter woke up, at least someone would be with her. We agreed that whatever time I finished up, I would just go back to her place to sleep until the morning. This way, we wouldn't have to wake up my daughter or cause her any unnecessary stress.

By 1:30 am, I had arrived and found the patrol officers knocking on apartment doors and escorting people away from the area. There was the heavy odor of gasoline emanating from the apartment building. Because the gasoline smell was so intense, I instructed headquarters to have all district fire companies respond, along with the first aid companies. The potential for this situation becoming an explosion was extremely likely, because a spark of any kind would be disastrous. The scene supervisor, Sergeant Bill Davis, instantly approached me and advised me that there was a man in his early thirties in the upstairs apartment, holding a five gallon can of gasoline. He had already doused himself in gasoline and poured it on the floors of his apartment and down the stairwell. He was threatening to ignite the gasoline if his demands weren't met. Davis told me the man was demanding to speak with a television crew or reporter so he could tell his side of the story. What that story was, we didn't know.

I asked Davis if any of the media had been notified. He shook his head and said, "No. We figured we would give you a try at him first."

He pointed to apartment 36B and warned, "Be careful. He's got a road flare. One spark and this place will go up like a Roman candle." I sarcastically thanked him for the advice, then noticed the name on the mailbox read Edward Styles. The front door was open and the stench of gasoline was everywhere. Before calling into the apartment, I removed my police windbreaker, put on a neighbor's jacket, and borrowed Davis' notepad, knowing that every good reporter carried one. I approached the front door of the building and a voice called out, "Are you from the TV station or the newspaper? You better not be a cop." If I said I was from the TV station, he would expect to see a camera crew, so I took a chance and told him that I was from the local radio station, WKRX. He asked me my name. Thinking fast, I told him my name was Frank Sayers, I was newly hired and was the on-call reporter, and that I wanted to hear his story. As I stood standing in a puddle of gasoline at the foyer landing, I saw a man standing in his underwear, holding an unlit road flare. The stairwell was obviously saturated with gasoline and the fumes were burning my eyes. He asked me to come up to talk, but I needed him to come down so we could grab him. Claiming that I was nervous and afraid and was having trouble breathing, I asked if he could meet me halfway down the stairs because I was having difficulty hearing him. He agreed and while we talked, I found out why he had gone off the deep end. As I took down notes, trying to appear authentic, he told me that he lost his job, his girlfriend of ten years left him for another guy, and he no longer had a reason to live. He had discovered that the guy she left him for was a friend from work and they had been carrying on an affair for the past year. He felt like he had been slapped in the face and was now being treated for depression. This was a combination that threw him over the edge.

As the man got more comfortable talking with me, I would slowly take one step back, which caused him to take another step forward toward the bottom of the stairs. I knew if I could get him to the doorway, the two officers standing on each side of the door outside could grab him and the flare. I eventually told him that I was getting nauseous from all the gas fumes and needed some fresh air. I asked him if it would be possible to continue our talk on the front porch. He agreed, "Okay, but no cops or I light this flare." As he stepped onto the porch, I quickly grabbed the flare and my two officers tackled him, pushed him to the ground, handcuffed him, and placed him under arrest. In a matter of seconds, it was over and nobody had gotten injured. I instructed Davis to go in and make sure there was no one else in the apartment. Inside, he found multiple cans of gasoline and empty pill containers on the kitchen table, with a note to the man's ex-girlfriend, stating that he was going to end his life.

Once I got back to my car, I was advised by headquarters to call Chief LaRocca and give him a briefing. When I stopped back at work, I called the chief at home and relayed to him that all went well, there were no problems, and we arrested one man, saying I would talk to him in the morning. It was now about 3:30 am, so I headed back home and slept at Kathleen's apartment until morning came. When my daughter woke up the next day, I told her I got called out late so Kathleen came over to stay with her. She didn't think twice about it and never knew what had happened the previous night or the danger that I had encountered.

CHAPTER 38
A COLD CASE

In the late 1970s when I was a sergeant, there was a certain homicide case that stayed with me for many years due to the violent and heinous nature and because our town had very few cases of this kind. It was a summer day when dispatch received a call from a neighbor to respond to a house at 326 West Culver Street for a wellness check because newspapers and mail had not been picked up in a few days. The owner of the home was an elderly woman in her eighties and lived by herself. She was always smiling and was extremely friendly. On any given day, you could find her working in her garden and whenever a patrol car drove by, she gave a friendly wave. She referred to us as her "boys" and every Christmas, she dropped off baked goods for the officers.

The first car to respond to the call was Officer Tolson, who had been on the job for less than five years. He not only noticed the newspapers and mail piled up, but he also observed a window on the side door that was broken, making him suspicious that this was probably a break-in. He immediately called me, since I was his supervisor, and advised me of the situation. I dispatched a second sector car to assist him and when the other unit arrived, both officers entered the house through the side door. They found that the house had been ransacked. Dresser drawers were open in one bedroom, couch and chair cushions had been removed and thrown onto the floor, lamps and collectibles were broken and thrown about, and the television in the living room was missing. Once the call was confirmed as a break-in, Officer Tolson followed protocol and radioed in, advising me to stop by. Within seconds, I received a second message on my beeper to respond with a 911 code attached, which meant to respond immediately. I knew right then and there that it was more than just a break-in.

Upon my arrival, I was met outside the front door by Tolson, who stated, "It's Mrs. Morrison. It appears that she has been murdered." I was incredulous. Who would want to kill this sweet woman? She didn't have a lot of money or valuable possessions. Tolson's next words were, "Boss, it's not a pretty sight. She has been brutally beaten with a broom." I turned and walked into the house with him, heading toward the back bedroom and seeing how her home had been trashed. In her bedroom, I found that her hands and feet were tied to the bedposts, her clothing had been removed, she was staring up at the ceiling, and she was covered in blood. I immediately backed out of the room and called for detectives. I had the officers secure the scene and told Tolson to begin an entry log, identifying the names and times of anyone that entered the crime scene.

During the next few hours, it was determined that someone broke into the house by way of a side door, raped, brutally assaulted, and killed Mrs. Morrison, and then ransacked the house to search for money and things of value. Officer Tolson worked with the detectives for the next several days, reviewing paperwork and speaking with neighbors and potential witnesses. The case turned cold due to the lack of suspects and any concrete evidence. However, Mrs. Morrison's granddaughter helped us to determine what might have been stolen and provided a list and pictures to the detectives. One of the stolen items was a

16" geisha doll with a red kimono. This stolen item would turn out to be a major piece of evidence that would ultimately help solve this case.

Jumping ahead fourteen years later, I was now the Detective Division Commander and Officer Tolson was now Detective Tolson, working a number of home invasion cases. One morning, he was dispatched to the scene of a burglary that had taken place. It was 10:00 am and I was at my morning staff meeting with the chief when my secretary called his office and stated my presence was needed at the burglary scene. The chief was annoyed that his meeting was disrupted, but I excused myself and went to the nearest phone, where I called Tolson. His phone rang twice and then I heard, "Boss, Tolson here. You need to respond to 655 Hidden Hills Lane right away." When I asked why, his reply was, "I can't talk on the phone, but you must respond immediately." Tolson was a senior detective and not prone to being excited very easily, so I knew something had him all worked up. I advised him I was on my way.

I arrived to find two patrol officers at the front door and one inside with Tolson. As I walked into the living room, Tolson was sitting at a table speaking with one of the homeowners, a young woman who looked to be in her late 20s. Seeing me, he stood up and handed me a folder, provided by the homeowner, with a list of items that may have been stolen. He then walked over to a nearby mantle that had pictures and decorative items on it. He gave me an icy stare, indicating that I should look closely at them. My first thought was, "Why am I here for a simple burglary and why am I looking at this mantle?" I was oblivious as to what I was supposed to be looking at until he tapped his fingers on the mantle next to one specific item. As I focused on it, I suddenly realized I was looking at a 16" geisha doll with a red kimono. There was an instant flashback to the Morrison murder. I immediately looked at the woman and commented what a beautiful doll it was. She replied, "Thank you. It is one of my most treasured gifts. My husband gave it to me years ago when we were first dating." As we were talking to the owner, Mrs. Monday, her husband Charles arrived home.

Detective Tolson introduced himself to Mr. Monday and assured him that his wife was fine. He then asked him to sit down and review the list of possible stolen items that his wife had given the police. We mentioned to him that we were just telling his wife how exquisite the geisha doll was and asked where he got it. A look of terror came over his face. He started to sweat, his hands began shaking, and he was staring blankly into space. I said, "I think you know why we are asking about the doll." After a long pause, his lips started moving but no sound came. He finally blurted out that he didn't mean to kill her, but she started scream-ing and said she was going to tell. He went out of control and tore off her clothes. He said that he saw a broom by the bed, picked it up, and struck her with it. Before he knew it, he was standing over her body, covered in blood. I advised him not to say another word and told Tolson, who already had his handcuffs out, to arrest the man and read him his rights.

It seemed that when Mr. Monday was about seventeen years old, he did odd jobs in Mrs. Morrison's neighborhood and often worked at her house. He had been questioned by the po-lice fourteen years before, but he had an alibi that was given by his mother, who was now deceased. He claimed that the murder was not premeditated and that he was looking to steal cash and other items that could be sold. When he unexpectedly encountered the woman in her home, he got scared and lost control. He later told us that he knew this day would even-tually come, but thought there was a statute of limitations on crimes. Unfortunately, there is none on a murder case. His defense attorney tried to have him charged as a juvenile since he was under the age of eighteen at the time of the offense, but because of the violent nature of the crime, the motion was denied. He was charged as an adult and found guilty. He was sentenced to life in prison at the state penitentiary.

CHAPTER 39
ARSON

Several high-profile cases occurred in our town that were of major significance. One of them dealt with the arson of a resident's home and was covered on the news stations and in the newspapers. Dispatch had received a call on Labor Day weekend that there was a house fire at Grover Street. This was in a residential neighborhood comprised of middle-income homes, most of which were split level. Police officers and fire companies were dispatched to the scene and found the house engulfed in flames. Fortunately, the firefighters got there quickly and were able to contain and extinguish the fire without damaging any of the surrounding homes. However, there was extensive interior damage to the house.

It was determined that the fire would be

cataloged as an arson case. Further investigation revealed that the homeowner and family members were away for the holiday weekend. Neighbors advised my detectives that there were a lot of teens and young adults in the home all weekend long who appeared to be partying. Pictures taken at the scene showed extensive graffiti on the walls that weren't burned by the fire, along with the destruction of furniture and appliances, plus large quantities of empty beer bottles. The walls that weren't burned were damaged with large holes, as if someone had taken a baseball bat to them.

We interviewed many people who lived on the street and said they initially didn't think anything of the loud music coming from the home because one of the homeowner's sons was in a band. They started getting suspicious when they saw a lot of unfamiliar cars parked on the street. Two witnesses wrote down several of the vehicle plate numbers and forwarded this information to us. That was when we caught our first break. The second one came when someone tried to cash a check that was stolen from the home. The lead detective picked up several potential suspects and began questioning them. We knew if we could get one suspect to cooperate, then it would cause a domino effect and allow us to get most, if not all, of the names of those that participated in the arson. During the questioning of one of our first suspects, we were told that the party had been planned and was called a "Bash Party." This was when a group of teenagers and young adults paid money to systematically destroy a home while under the influence of alcohol and drugs. When asked how people knew that the house would be empty for the weekend, we were told that the teenage son who lived there had mentioned to friends that he and his family were going away.

Subsequently, with all the information that was accumulated from interviews, arrests were made, including charging eight adults and fourteen juveniles, ranging from burglary to arson. Some of the lesser charges were criminal mischief, trespassing, and consumption of alcohol by a minor. Ironically, before this incident, I had conducted a seminar in our civic center that dealt with the Neighborhood Watch Program. Because of the success of this program and the cooperation of so many residents, along with the diligent work of my detectives, the case was solved quickly.

CHAPTER 40
THE PSYCHOTHERAPIST

In 1999, my oldest son Chris, after having graduated several years earlier from a university in Florida with a degree in Criminal Justice, decided to switch career paths and informed me that he wanted to follow in my footsteps by joining law enforcement. After a lengthy testing program that included a written test, psychological and oral interviews, and a physical fitness test, he was hired by the same police department in which I served and where I was now Chief of Detectives. He entered the police academy for a twenty-six-week program and received training in all aspects of police work. Midway through his academy class, there was a family night where recruits were required to bring one family member. It could be a spouse, parent, sibling, cousin, or fiancée. This night would give the family members a better understanding of the physical and psychological stresses that would accompany police officers in their career. My son asked me if I would represent him as a family member. I had served on the job for more than thirty years at that point and thought he should ask his mother since I was all too familiar with the dangers of this career. However, he persisted and I reluctantly agreed to go. Ironically, my friend and academy classmate, Joe Morris, was also asked to go because his son was in the same academy class as mine, and both were hired by the same department.

Neither Joe nor I wanted to attend because we both felt it would be a waste of time, but we went anyway in support of our sons. As we arrived and entered the building, we saw rows of rectangular tables with chairs behind them for family members to sit. There were pads and pens at each table in case anyone wanted to take notes. In the front of the room was a large desk and behind that was a huge blackboard with the name Stephanie Samuels written on it. We purposely sat in the last row in the back of the room because we didn't want to get called on to participate in any line of questioning. I had no idea what to expect from this instructor and didn't know what she looked like, but my son informed me that she liked to drop the F-bomb and had a mouth like a truck driver. I had started to conceive a mental picture of what she might look like and I imagined a woman in her late fifties, with a hard weathered look, unkempt appearance, and no style with respect to her fashion wardrobe. Shortly after the group was settled down, Stephanie Samuels, a psychotherapist, was introduced.

As she stepped to the front of the room, I saw this very attractive woman in her mid-thirties, with short brown hair, nicely dressed, and physically fit – the complete opposite of what I had envisioned in my mind. I could tell by the murmuring in the crowd that most people thought as I did and expected someone completely different. My son had prepared me for the language I was about to hear, so I wasn't shocked when she dropped the F-bomb ten times in the first three minutes. However, I can't say that the others were prepared. Stephanie certainly got their attention very quickly. Joe and I found her to be hilarious and entertaining, but weren't getting anything out of her speech. For the next half hour, we barely listened to her and commented to each other about what a waste of time this was. We were cracking jokes, watching the clock, and hoping she would show a movie. We noticed her glaring at us every now and then, indicating that she was aware of our inattentiveness. Suddenly, her words started to resonate. I was beginning to as if this woman, who I had never met before, personally knew me and my life story because the words she was speaking mirrored my life for the past thirty years. It was very unsettling to hear her describe the innermost feelings that had plagued me for such a long time. Joe continued to make comments, but I was now intently listening and told him to shut up because I wanted to hear more of what she had to say.

For the next hour, I listened as she talked about marital problems among police officers; I could relate because I had two failed marriages and was engaged to be married for the third time. She also spoke about officers having mood swings because of the horrific things they saw every day on a regular basis. Alcoholism was also a topic discussed because some police officers drank to try and forget what they had seen on the job. She spoke of cops having so many family problems because they wanted to shelter their loved ones from the details of the ugliness around them, leaving family members feeling shut out when in essence, the officers just wanted to spare and protect them.

As her presentation came to an end, I was compelled to let Stephanie Samuels know how amazed I was that she knew my life so well. I was beginning to understand that her practice focused on counseling police officers and first responders through the most difficult times in their lives and she understood the complexity of what we had to endure throughout our careers. It certainly helped me to realize why the suicide rate among police officers was so high. Before leaving for the evening, I managed to spend a few private minutes with her, discussing some of the problems I had experienced. Her advice was to set up an appointment to meet in her office, where we could sit down and continue the conversation in depth. I thanked her for her time and told her that if she ever needed my help, to let me know and I would be there.

During my first session with Stephanie, we discussed many critical incidents that I had experienced on the job. This is when she explained that many police officers suffered from PTSD or Post Traumatic Stress Disorder, which is a mental health condition that is triggered by experiencing or witnessing horrific or terrifying events. She told me of the symptoms, which included flashbacks, nightmares, and anxiety, all of which I had experienced from time to time. In my following sessions with her, it became clearer that I might have this condition. Certain triggers could bring on the onset and in my case, it was and continues to be fevers. When my body reaches a high fever, I suddenly get flashbacks of critical incidents that occurred on the job. For the longest time, my flashbacks were of Jennifer McCauley, the little girl who was struck by a school bus and died in my arms.

The benefits of these counseling sessions were giving me the ability to cope with this disorder. As time went on, I was able to work with Stephanie at the police academy, teaching recruits and family members about the long-term effects of PTSD. On one such occasion, Stephanie asked me if I would bring my new wife, Kathleen, to family night at the police academy, where we could be guest speakers. Stephanie separated everyone into two groups, one being recruits and the other being the family members. She thought that the recruits would benefit from my thirty or more years on the job and that Kathleen could give the family members some insight into the life of a police officer from a spouse and civilian's perspective.

Little did I know, when I met Stephanie

Samuels for the first time at the police academy family night, the profound effect she would have on me for the rest of my life. Just when I started working through the effects of the loss of Jennifer McCauley and was able to put that incident to rest, the ultimate critical incident occurred. It happened on September 11, 2001.

CHAPTER 41
SEPTEMBER 11, 2001

I had been seeing Stephanie Samuels, the psychotherapist, for over a year and was starting to come to terms with the effects of PTSD and the critical incidents I had experienced throughout my career. I never suspected that the ultimate critical incident was right around the corner. There are historical events that have happened where most people remember exactly where they were at the time. For example, my father always told me that on December 7, 1941, he was relaxing at home, reading the Sunday newspaper and listening to the radio, when he heard that Pearl Harbor had been attacked. I also remember that on November 22, 1963, when I heard the news that John F. Kennedy was assassinated, I was in my senior year of high school, sitting in English class. I also remember that on September 11,

2001, when the World Trade Center in New York City was attacked by terrorists, I was just starting my morning at work.

It was about 8:30 am when I got to work and it had begun like any other beautiful September day. I picked up my morning coffee and reported to my new office at the Special Operations Precinct, which is where the county had turned a two-mile stretch of beach into a county park. Stepping out of my office and onto the deck that was attached, I could smell the crisp, clean air with the breeze coming off the water. It was wonderfully refreshing and looking across Raritan Bay, I could view the beautiful New York City skyline that I had seen so many times before. However, there was something unusual about this day because I noticed considerable smoke billowing from the upper floors of one of the Trade Center towers across the bay. My first thought was, "How do you fight a fire that high up?" That's when my dispatcher called out to tell me that television reports were saying a plane had crashed into one of the towers. Not knowing yet that this was a terrorist attack, I remember wondering how a sightseeing plane or helicopter could crash into this monstrous building. As the news coverage continued on television, we began getting swamped with phone calls from residents, asking what was going on. Not knowing much, we told callers to stay calm and that as more information was given to us, it would be relayed to them. Within minutes of initially noticing the smoke from one tower, I went back into the office to get my binoculars. Returning to the outside deck, I could now see that both towers were on fire. There was a large group of residents standing outside our precinct, concerned that we were at war. I did my best to calm them down, but still checked on the condition of the towers while staring through my binoculars. Just then, Sergeant Skip Reed, who was the patrol supervisor working the nearby area, pulled into the precinct and asked if I had gotten any further information on what was happening. Having no further information other than the second tower being hit by a plane shortly after the first, he asked to borrow my binoculars. I was still attempting to deal with the large crowd that had gathered when I glanced down at my watch, noticing it was just about 10:00 am.

I heard Sergeant Reed calling me from the deck, urging me to come right away. His face appeared very pale and he started mumbling words that I couldn't make sense of. The only thing I could understand him say was,

"It's gone." He handed me the binoculars and pointed toward the towers. As I looked through them, I could see that one of the towers was gone. It had collapsed. There was now twice as much smoke – clouds billowing with heavy white smoke that were blowing toward Brooklyn and then out to sea. All I could think was, "Oh my God." Then I heard my dispatcher call out again, telling me that Chief LaRocca was on the phone. Simultaneously, my beeper was registering 911 emergency messages. I quickly ran into the building, picked up the phone, and called the chief, who instructed me to report to headquarters immediately. I hurried into my car and headed back to meet him while still listening to the radio for more news updates. While en route, I learned that the second tower, the North Tower, had just come down. It was now approximately 10:30 am.

At the chief's office, all five of us division commanders were there. Chief LaRocca, looking somber, informed us that requests from the NYPD had gone out, asking for all available manpower and any anti-terrorist units to respond. Since I had been trained and had gone to so many schools regarding terrorism, it was only logical that my unit would be sent. He asked me if I was prepared to go and I told him I was, but asked who would be joining me since some of my men were unavailable. He told me that a new unit was being assembled as we spoke, comprised of one lieutenant, three sergeants, and fourteen patrol officers, all of whom were not scheduled to work for the next few days. I was told to meet them in the parking lot, where we kept our forty-two-foot Mobile Command Center, which looked like a very long RV. It contained bays of portable radios, first aid equipment, riot gear, computers, oxygen masks, face masks, and Scott Air Packs, which were open circuit, self-contained breathing apparatuses that were mostly used by firefighters. Captain Steiner, who was the patrol division commander, gave me a list of who I would be commanding. I recognized all of the names of the men I would be working with, but I was deeply concerned about one man; not because of his ability to do the job, but because of personal reasons. Namely, the fact that he was my youngest son and had only been on the job for a few months. Once all the men were assembled, I gave them as much information that was available at that point. I had no idea how long we would be in the city and what we were about to endure. I only knew that my confidence level in their abilities to complete this assignment would never be in doubt.

I had each man notify their families that we would be going to New York to assist with the rescue of possible victims and didn't know how long we would be gone. Upon leaving head-quarters, my instructions were clear and they were to assemble at the County Police and Fire Academy to await further instructions. Within one hour after reaching the academy, additional manpower consisting of almost two hundred fifty police officers from surrounding towns and counties arrived. We all left in a caravan of trucks and buses, along with our Mobile Command Center, to the Staten Island Ferry, where we were taken across the water to assist in the rescue and help relieve officers who had been there since the morning hours. It was eerily silent on the ferry and all we heard was the sound of waves crashing against the side and front of the boat. Not one word was spoken by any officer on our ride over, most-ly because we were all in shock and couldn't comprehend the magnitude of the nightmare that had just begun.

Looking across the Hudson River to New York, all we could see were shades of black and gray from the smoke and shades of orange and red flickering from the burning buildings, accompanied by huge clouds of dust filling the sky. When the silence had broken, one of my younger officers pointed toward the buildings and, with a nervous voice, asked if we were going in. I gathered all of my team to one side and told them, "Listen to me good. Stay together, rely on your training, pay attention to what's going on around you, and help as many people as you can. You're going to see some terrible sights. Work through them and be safe." The ferry let us off down by Wall Street, where some buses took us to a mustering area to receive our next assignments.

Our first assignment was to assist the National Guard in setting up a perimeter around Ground Zero, the immediate area where the towers came down. Our perimeter was about a ten-block-square area and this was done because stores and businesses were being looted. The visibility was practically zero because the entire area was filled with heavy, dense black smoke and dust that covered all of us. Within the hour, I had been approached by an NYPD officer who I believed to be at least a captain, but was unsure because he was filthy and covered head to toe in black dust. He asked me who was in charge and I informed him of my rank and that I was. He also asked how many people I had under my command. I told him that I had almost forty men that included the eighteen in my unit and other officers from the ferry that were assigned to me from neighboring towns. He asked that I take half of the men and proceed to Liberty and Church Streets, which was right in the middle of Ground Zero, to assist in rescues. As requested, I took my men moving forward and left the others that had been assigned to me to continue securing the perimeter.

Walking from our current location to our new assignment area that was about six blocks away was extremely difficult. We were walking through water-covered streets from ruptured hydrants and building sprinkler systems that had gone off, along with debris and dust that blanketed the ground with a paste-like material that clung to our boots, giving us the feeling that our boots were covered in paper mache. Every so often, we had to stop to remove the large amounts of debris from our boots that made them feel so heavy. At the corner of Broadway and Vesey Street, we encountered some firefighters and a battalion chief who diverted us because of the enormous amount of debris blocking the road ahead of us. This included parked and demolished cars, glass, and brick chunks that had fallen from buildings. They suggested that we walk down Vesey Street to Church Street and continue until we got to Liberty Street.

Halfway down Vesey Street, on the sidewalk, we found an engine that appeared to come from one of the jets that had hit the World Trade Center. We marked it off in yellow crime scene tape and continued to Church Street. When we reached the corner of Vesey and Church, looking to the right, we could see Building Seven of the World Trade Center, an approximate fifty-story building that had collapsed and fallen on its side, giving the appearance of now being just a seven-story building. I couldn't imagine how this building collapsed when it was a distance away from the Twin Towers.

Shortly after turning onto Church Street, we immediately thought that we were about to enter the Gates of Hell. We could feel the intense heat that was emanating from buildings three and four. The steel girders that had at one time held these buildings together were now glowing red and bent into pretzel-like shapes from the enormous heat that was causing them to melt. The sights of burning buildings were only compounded by the smell of smoke and burning flesh. This was a smell that would stay with me for the rest of my life. Ahead of us, we could see scorched and abandoned police cars, fire trucks, and emergency service vehicles. Our eyes were burning from the dust and glass that was in the air and our chests felt heavy, making it difficult to breathe due to the toxic air that we took in. We continued forward, reaching Trinity Church. That's when we saw a wrought-iron fence that enclosed the rear of the church. We found what appeared to have once been a firefighter. On the ground, there was an empty shell of a fireman's jacket that was badly burned, an empty helmet, and a pair of work gloves. I could only imagine that this firefighter had turned away to protect himself from the blast of the fireball that emanated from the ignited jet fuel and was burning buildings three and four, but because the heat was so extreme, he ultimately lost his life and probably disintegrated. The mass destruction that surrounded us reminded me of the pictures I had seen of cities that were destroyed by bombings in World War II.

As I took in this terrible sight all around me, my eyes became fixed on the church. I was silently asking God to take care of my people and to get us through the days to come. At that moment, I couldn't help but notice that the stained glass windows in the church had not been broken. They were completely intact and I immediately felt a sense of calm that came over me because my faith was strong and I knew that God would protect us. Minutes later, we arrived at our assigned location, which was at Liberty and Church Streets.

The area around One Liberty Plaza was covered in massive quantities of debris. I wondered what to do next because we were initially told to assist with rescues, but no one was there to give us direction. From out of the dust and debris came two doctors from Harlem Hospital, along with a triage unit made up of eight to ten medical staff members. The doctors told us they were sent to set up a mobile triage unit, which is designed to respond to a mass casualty incident, and prepare for victims with injuries. The most logical place would have been the ground floor of One Liberty Plaza, but with so much destruction blocking the entrances to the stores, we couldn't possibly get in without removing debris. I instructed my unit to assist the doctors and to remove as much debris as they could from that area. Within moments, everyone was digging in and getting rid of cement pieces from the buildings that had hit the ground and smashed, most weighing between ten and fifty pounds. Once we secured a safe path into the building, we discovered it was the Brooks Brothers store. We knew we had the perfect place to set up, but we had to remove all the merchandise on the first floor.

It took my men approximately one hour to move everything out from the store and into the street. While this was being done, I had run into a fire chief who was asking where we were from and thanking us. As I returned to one of the cleared areas, I noticed what appeared to be piles of bodies. I was speechless because I couldn't believe that my men would be so disrespectful by not properly laying them out. Fortunately, as I got closer, I realized that this pile was well-dressed store mannequins. I breathed a sigh of relief. The ground floor was now clear, the doctors had set up their triage unit, and we anxiously waited for many injured victims to arrive.

At this point, I divided my unit into two eight-man teams, each consisting of one sergeant and seven officers, keeping one sergeant with me. My lieutenant was still in Staten Island at the ferry with the Mobile Command Center. We were waiting for clearance to bring that over. My instructions to both teams were to assist the rescue units digging through the rubble in search of possible victims. From my vantage point at One Liberty Plaza, I could hear the constant droning of heavy machinery, digging in the rubble, being careful not to disturb too much of the pile so as not to cause a cave-in. It was a sickening sound and the odor of the diesel fuel mixed with the smell of jet fuel and death was causing me to be nauseous. Through all of this and watching the rescue workers climbing into the crevices of rubble, desperately trying to find victims, I felt as if I was watching the actions of live heroes. Every once in a while, it became deathly silent except for when we heard the sound of a horn blasting, which indicated that someone was found. At that moment, the machinery would stop and everyone would rush to that area and begin removing pieces of concrete and debris. We would all anxiously wait to hear whether we recovered a victim that was alive. When an orange body bag was requested, we knew right then that a victim had perished. As the hours passed by, more and more orange bags were called for. It was obvious from where we were, and after seeing what was being done, that the odds of rescuing any victims were slim and what initially started as a rescue mission had now become a recovery one.

As time went on, the men became more and more exhausted but they refused to stop and never gave up. While I was back at the triage unit, a fire chief arrived and told me and the doctors there was a possibility that there were some victims alive and trapped in a subway platform that ran underneath what was once the Trade Center. There was still a visible entryway from Church Street and I was asked if there was available manpower to check it out. I pulled one of my teams from the rescue area to go into the subway and see if anyone was there and possibly still alive. At the subway area with my men, we encountered a large gate blocking our way. There was no way we were going to get past it, so I requested some heavy construction cutting tools from some workers right outside the entrance in order to get the gate down. Once it was removed, we started down into the subway, following some stairs that led to the platform. We searched and called out for people, but there was only silence. It was pitch black except for the light that came from our flashlights, and we had to rely on sounds to help in our search. This continued for about thirty minutes without any positive results. Just as I was telling my men that it was time to get back out, we heard a terrible rumble that was causing pieces of concrete to dislodge and fall into the subway. I immediately told them to get out as quickly as possible and everyone ran to get to safety. Once outside, I gave a headcount to see if they were all accounted for. Two men were missing, one being my son. Turning to go back, we heard a thunderous crash and the entrance collapsed, leaving us no way to get back in. I assumed the worst and believed my son and another officer had just been killed. I didn't know that when the debris in the subway was falling, they had gotten separated from the others and exited from a second entrance that we were unaware of. As I was trying to come to terms with the fact that I might have just lost two officers, I heard some of the men yell out, "Look who's coming from the other side of the street!" There they were, strolling up Church Street like it was a Sunday afternoon back home. My first instinct was to hug them both. My second was to punch them in the face for not staying with the group. Needless to say, they got hugs and not punches. I was just happy to see them. This was the perfect opportunity to stress why they all had to stay together.

It had been an extremely long day and we were all sitting at the bottom of the steps of One Liberty Plaza. Our eyes were burning and we were told not to rub our eyes due to the glass particles from building windows that were mixed in with the black dust in the air. We were taken by a fire rescue unit to a fire hydrant that was turned into an eyewash station. One by one, we all had our eyes flushed and wiped clean. We returned to One Liberty Plaza soaking wet, especially our feet. Out of nowhere appeared about five or six young adults, who looked like they were in their late teens or early twenties, wearing yellow reflective vests and carrying a large box. We couldn't possibly imagine how they got into the area because security was tight and only police officers, firefighters, and rescue workers were allowed in. They approached us and without saying a word, they began unlacing our boots. We were all too tired to ask them why. They then removed our boots and socks, and from out of their box, they put brand new perfectly clean and dry socks on our feet. They put our boots back on, retied them, and within moments were gone. My men were in shock, but I was able to thank these angels of mercy for the kindness they showed. To this day, I still remember one member of that group. He had a kind face, a bright smile, and wore a red bandana tied around his neck. We never saw them again.

Our feet were now dry, our eyes were flushed clean, and we were exhausted. We hadn't eaten any food or drank any water since before we arrived in New York City. The dust and smoke still hung heavy in the air, not allowing us to see the sky and making it difficult to distinguish between night and day. The orange bags continued to arrive at the triage unit and still there were no live victims. It was becoming very frustrating because we weren't rescuing anybody. Instead, we were finding and cataloging body parts or remains of the victims. The strain on my men was becoming unbearable. I don't know how they maintained their purpose for being there, but they were consummate professionals throughout our time there. One of my younger officers, who had just been relieved from working with the doctors, said with tears in his eyes, "I don't know if I can continue doing this." I put my arms on his shoulders and reminded him that we were assigned to do a job and although it was sad and difficult, we had to move on and continue.

I told one of my detectives to scour the area for any food or drinks. Across the street from Liberty Plaza was a Burger King that had been abandoned, with broken windows and a considerable amount of debris in front of it. He went in to investigate if there was anything edible inside the restaurant. Returning within minutes, he advised me that one of the freezers was not damaged and there were bottles of water and food. I immediately sent the rest of my unit and some nearby rescue workers to that area, where they could get some food and nourishment. Inside the freezer, they found boxes of cooked hamburger patties, rolls, and condiments. One of the rescue workers had a cadaver dog with him, so he fed the dog beef patties. Another rescue worker made a ketch-up sandwich on rolls. All the other men sat on the floor, eating burgers and tomatoes that they found in a nearby box. After a short time, I saw my men come back, carrying boxes of food to distribute to the doctors and any other workers they may have met up with along the way. When they reached me, they gave me a double burger sandwich with cheese and to-mato, one that they had made themselves. I remember how good it tasted and had a much better respect for fast food after that.

With an enormous amount of manpower and heavy equipment digging into the pile and looking for victims, we were able to check the surrounding area for anyone who might be trapped in other buildings. We en-countered a young fireman who was sitting in the back of an abandoned emergency ser-vice truck. He told us he was from either the Bronx or Brooklyn and while responding to the Trade Center earlier in the day, the truck he was in had overheated. His captain told him to stay with the truck and to get on the next available unit that passed by. Looking at his face, you could see the exhaustion of a man that had been utterly defeated. He had the look of despair written all over him. When we saw him, the entire surrounding area was gray and white from smoke and dust, but we could still make out the yellow stripes on his once black EMS or fireman's jacket, while his helmet lay nearby. Above him, we could see a detached pole with a rectangular sign that read TOWER LADDER in white lettering and the number 15 in yellow. We talked to him for about fifteen minutes while he told us his story. He relayed to us that he believed everyone in his company had died because he had heard on the radio that his unit was one of the first to arrive and they went into the buildings. He later heard on the radio that both towers had come down, convincing him of the worst. When another group of firemen arrived, they told us they would take care of the man, so we left and continued on our search.

We checked any abandoned cars and buildings that were accessible, seeking live victims, but we were unable to locate any. We worked our way back to the triage unit and I had my forensic photographer take pictures of everything we saw so they could be forwarded to the FBI. He was very uncomfortable taking pictures of this mass destruction, but I reminded him that the pictures he was taking were evidence and would assist in the investigation of this tragedy. After all, wasn't this the ultimate crime scene?

We worked through the night, but when morning came we couldn't tell what time it was because the sun was blocked out by the smoke and dust and our watches were constantly covered with heavy grime. Although communications were down through cellular service, I was able to communicate with my Mobile Command Center by way of portable radio. I was advised that the NYPD was going to try to get our command center onto one of the ferries and bring it across the water. About an hour later, I received a call on my radio from my lieutenant, who was with the command center, reporting that they were on their way. Once they arrived, they received an escort up Broadway to Liberty Street, where it would stay. The sight of our command center was a shot in the arm for our morale. We knew there would be blankets, a change of clothes, water, and other essentials that we knew would come in handy. I took all my men inside and every bit of floor space was used so they could get some needed rest for about an hour. They then left and continued their search for victims. I had been receiving sporadic messages through the command center from the chief, wanting to know our position, if anyone had been injured, and if we were still needed there. Because other units were being relieved regularly, he thought it best that our unit was relieved as well since we were needed back in our hometown. I gathered my men and asked if they wanted to stay and continue or to be relieved. Every one of them wanted to stay. I was so proud of them for that. Peering up at the sky at that moment, the dust and smoke were just starting to dissipate and we could finally see a patch of blue sky. We took this as a sign that our decision to stay was the right one. I relayed to the chief that we wanted to stay but after thinking about it for a while, he determined that it was best for us to be relieved and come home. Shortly after that, the Red Cross showed up and distributed hot food, fresh water, and clean clothes to everyone working. An NYPD deputy inspector met me at the command center and thanked us for everything that we had done since arriving and for sharing the command center with his people so communications could be better. Within the hour, all my officers were in the command center and headed back to the ferry. My men were angry that we were called back by the chief because they felt their presence was needed in New York City, but I explained that we followed orders and those were that we were to return home. So that is what we did.

The ferry ride home was difficult. We were sad and angry and as we all looked back at the city, we felt like we were abandoning our brothers and sisters who had not been found and were still lying beneath the rubble that was once the World Trade Center. We stopped and said a silent prayer to have God watch over all those left behind and to keep them safe. When we returned to headquarters, the chief was waiting for us. He thanked every one of us for our service and dismissed us to go home to be with our families.

I was still filthy, but I wanted and needed to see my wife, Kathleen. She was a teacher working at the town's middle school and was privately tutoring students after work. Having not been able to communicate with her while in New York, I knew she had to be a wreck. The only information she knew was what she saw on television from the news updates. I can't imagine what she must have gone through, wondering if we were injured during our search for victims or if we were even alive. I immediately drove to the middle school, parked the car, and walked through the hallway that led directly to her classroom. I was never so happy to see my wife and as soon as our eyes locked, we ran into each other's arms and hugged with tears in our eyes. That hug seemed to last an eternity and after what my men and I had been through, I didn't want to let go. After several minutes, she asked me what I needed and who I wanted to be with. I told her I wanted to be with her and her parents. She told me to go home and get myself cleaned up, then called her parents and told them to cancel any plans because we would be getting together with them, per my request. When we met up later, I did a lot of crying as I recalled my experience for the last two days. They calmly listened, let me speak when I was ready, and allowed me to get my tears out as I told my story. I was so blessed to not only survive this nightmare, but to have a family that loved and wholeheartedly supported me.

Years have gone by and I still remember the details of my time at Ground Zero. The nightmares have continued and I will forever hold onto the names and faces of everyone that I encountered after America was attacked. I remember being a young boy and looking into my father's eyes when he would watch movies or television shows about Pearl Harbor. The tears would roll down his cheeks and I would ask, "Why are you crying? The war is over and you're fine." He would look at me, putting his hands on my face, and answer, "When this happens to you, and I hope to God it never does, you will understand why I cry." I never quite understood just what he meant until September 11, 2001. Now, tears roll down my cheeks as I try to explain to my grandchildren why I cry.

CHAPTER 42
END OF WATCH

The effects of September 11, 2001 weighed heavily on me. With the accumulation of many critical incidents that had plagued me over my career, I was still receiving counseling. After a personal tragedy in 2004, when my wife's mother and godmother were killed in a motor vehicle accident, I started considering retirement. I wasn't sure how much more I could take, so in 2005, I decided to put in my papers and officially end my journey in law enforcement after serving my town for almost thirty-seven years.

Because I now had a much better understanding of the effects of PTSD, I wanted to offer my support to Stephanie Samuels, the psychotherapist and founder of the non-profit organization called COPLINE, an anonymous helpline that gives law enforcement officers across the country a place to discuss their feelings anonymously. Since I had experienced so many critical incidents and knew so many other officers did, as well, I eagerly accepted Stephanie's offer when she asked me to serve as an executive board member for COPLINE.

My twenty-year relationship with Stephanie and the counseling she has provided has helped me to effectively deal with PTSD. I still have triggers, such as the smell of a fire, watching a bomb explode in a movie scene, or even passing a motor vehicle accident, that bring me back to some of the worst critical incidents in my life. This disorder will probably stay with me forever, but with the support of other officers, my family, and friends, I can confront my demons in a non-destructive way.

When I reflect on my career, I think back to the many challenges that I've faced and the opportunities that granted me the ability to change lives for the better. As we all pass through this world, we leave footprints that become our legacies. I can only hope that the footprints that I have left have created a positive effect on those that I've encountered. I envision every incident that has defined my life as bricks in a wall. Some are small and some are large, but we all cast our shadow on that wall.

CPSIA information can be obtained
at www.ICGtesting.com
Printed in the USA
FSHW021340111020
74692FS